In Your
KITCHEN!

In Your
**BACK
YARD!**

SUPER COOL

SCIENCE

EXPERIMENTS

FOR KIDS

Over 50 fun projects to try at home

CHARTWELL
BOOKS

Inspiring | Educating | Creating | Entertaining

Brimming with creative inspiration, how-to projects, and useful information to enrich your everyday life, Quarto Knows is a favorite destination for those pursuing their interests and passions. Visit our site and dig deeper with our books into your area of interest: Quarto Creates, Quarto Cooks, Quarto Homes, Quarto Lives, Quarto Drives, Quarto Explores, Quarto Gifts, or Quarto Kids.

© 2020 Quarto Publishing plc

This edition published in 2020 by Chartwell Books,
an imprint of The Quarto Group,
142 West 36th Street, 4th Floor
New York, NY 10018 USA
T (212) 779-4972 F (212) 779-6058
www.QuartoKnows.com

Contains content originally published in 2020 as
Experiment with Outdoor Science and in 2019 as *Experiment
with Kitchen Science* by QED Publishing, an imprint of
The Quarto Group, The Old Brewery, 6 Blundell Street,
London N7 9BH, United Kingdom.

10 9 8 7 6 5 4 3

ISBN: 978-0-7858-3896-8

Printed in China

Chartwell titles are also available at discount for retail, wholesale, promotional, and bulk purchase. For details, contact the Special Sales Manager by email at specialsales@quarto.com or by mail at The Quarto Group, Attn: Special Sales Manager, 100 Cummings Center Suite 265D, Beverly, MA 01915, USA.

Publisher: Rage Kindelsperger
Creative Director: Laura Drew
Editorial Director: Pauline Molinari
Managing Editor: Cara Donaldson
Project Editor: Cathy Davis
Cover Design: James Kegley
Interior Design and Editorial: Starry Dog Books Ltd
Illustrator: Giulia Zoavo
Consultant: Pete Robinson

All photographs by Starry Dog Books Ltd
with the exception of the following:

Alamy: 23 tilt&shift / Stockimo / Alamy Stock Photo

Fiona Haye: 36-37

Shutterstock: 8-9 b/g thidaphon taoha; 10-11 b/g ifong;
14-15 b/g sumroeng chinnapan; 16-17 b/g Evgeny Atamanenko;
18-19 b/g Pipochka; 33 epsylon_lyrae, 33 b/g Pooh photo;
35b (clockwise from top) a) domnitsky, b) Tamara Kulikova,
c) Nipaporn Panyacharoen; 38-39 NewAfrica, 39tl oksana2010,
39tc oksana2010; 42-43 Sergei Mironenko; 46/47 b/g keeplight;
49 Andreas Hvidsten; 56-57 b/g cooperr; 58-59 b/g Vivo e verde;
62-63 b/gd1sk, 63b jannoon028; 66 (hand) Bloomicon, 66 b/g
Erkki Makkonen. 76 b/g D. Pimborough; 78 b/g Eldorado
SuperVector; 82 Oxy_gen; 86 b/g thidaphon taoha; 90 b/gCK
Foto; 92 b/g Anusorn Nakdee; 98 b/g Olga Hmelevskaya;
102 b/g white snow; 104 b/g mim.girl; 115 zkruger,
124 Svetlana Foote; 124 Moving Moment; 124 Olga Popova;
126 Ryzhkov Photography.

Superstock: 31 Radius

CONTENTS

CHAPTER 4: BUGS AND BIRDS

CHAPTER 5: SKY AND SPACE

CHAPTER 6: MAD MIXTURES

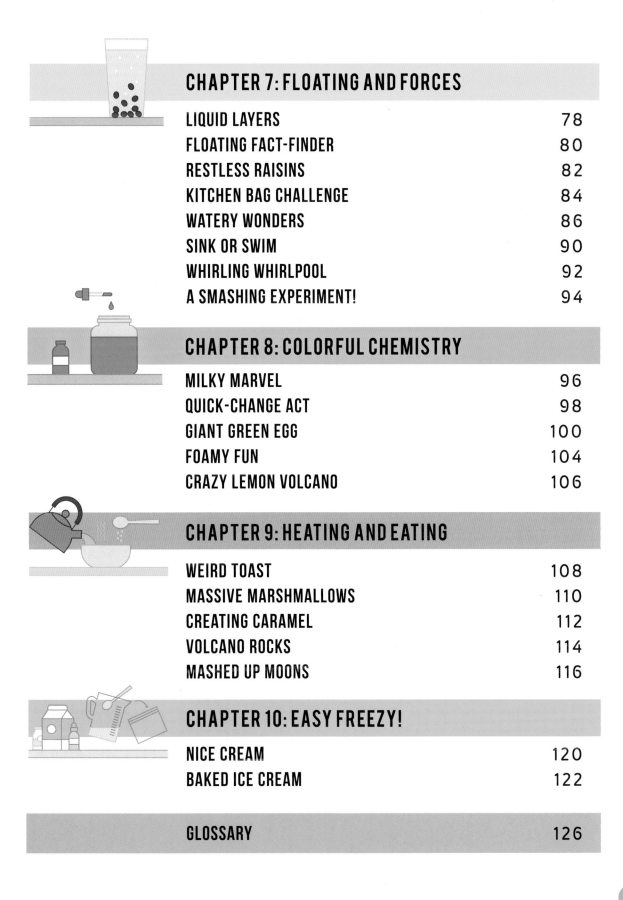

CHAPTER 7: FLOATING AND FORCES

CHAPTER 8: COLORFUL CHEMISTRY

CHAPTER 9: HEATING AND EATING

CHAPTER 10: EASY FREEZY!

INTRODUCTION

The world's biggest science lab is right outside your window. Yes, the great outdoors is full of moving things, living things, and wild weather. Science is about everything. It's even about food and drink. This book is full of BIG science experiments, maximum mess, and shout-out-loud FUN! And you even get to EAT some of your experiments! Let's get started...

Golden rules
FOR SENSIBLE SCIENTISTS

Rule 1
BE ORGANIZED
Before you start an experiment, read the instructions and make sure you have everything you need to hand.

Look out for the handy hints in circles—they will help to make the experiments work.

Rule 2
BE SAFE!
Ask for adult help whenever you see this symbol. Always follow the WARNING! advice in the red boxes. Don't go anywhere alone, especially at night. Don't eat wild plants; they may be toxic. Don't handle creatures such as bugs or spiders unless an adult has told you they're safe. Never experiment with flames, mains electricity, or gas. Always ask an adult to do any cutting.

ASK AN ADULT

 WARNING! Water may spill at stage 4.

Rule 3
BE TIDY!
Tidy up after each experiment and throw away or recycle waste materials. Look for the yellow MESS WARNING! boxes and follow the advice.

 MESS WARNING! Food coloring stains—wear old clothes!

You can try these experiments in any order, but the science explanations make more sense if you tackle them in the order they appear in this book. What's certain is that wherever you start, you're sure to get a taste for kitchen and outdoor science!

READY – STEADY – EXPERIMENT!

You can find out about the science words in **bold** in the glossary on pages 126-128.

THINK GREEN AND RECYCLE!

Many of the projects in this book provide a great way to recycle plastic items; wherever possible, try and find the items you need at home rather than buying new products. When you have finished, recycle any plastic items. That way you can help to keep plastic out of landfills..

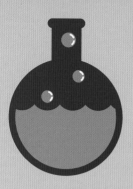

FLOAT YOUR BOATS

Enjoy a boat trip in your own backyard with a bobbing bottle boat and, on the next page, a folded paper boat that floats!

> ⚠️ **WARNING!**
> DON'T float your boats in ponds, rivers, lakes, or canals.

1 Ask an adult to make a cut (A) in the side of a 16.9 ounce (500 ml) plastic bottle. Cut out the rest of the rectangle.

ASK AN ADULT

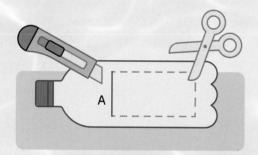

2 Use packing tape to attach a pen to the opposite side of the bottle.

The pen must be straight and exactly in the center of the uncut side.

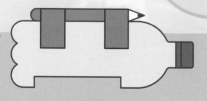

3 Roll a 1-inch (2.5 cm) wide ball of modeling clay and press it into the boat, making sure it's in the center. Stick a drinking straw into the modeling clay and secure it with thin tape.

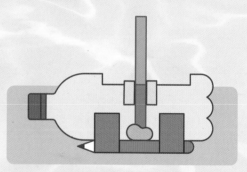

4 To make the sail, cut the end off a short envelope. Use a sharp pencil to make a hole in the uncut end, then slide the envelope onto the straw.

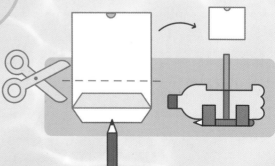

You will need...

- 16.9 ounce (500 ml) plastic screw-top bottle
- Knife
- Scissors
- Pen
- Packing tape
- Modeling clay
- Drinking straw
- Tape
- Short envelope
- Sharp pencil

5 Your boat is ready to launch. If it leans to one side on the water, simply straighten the mast until the boat is upright. Blow gently on the sail to move the boat along.

Float your boat in a wading pool or large container of water.

The Science:
FLOATING

A force called gravity pushes the boat down into the water, but the water pushes back just as hard: this is a force called upthrust. Your boat floats, or is **buoyant**, because the water it pushes aside weighs the same as the boat.

You can make a paper boat by folding just one sheet of paper! Then have fun decorating it.

You will need...

- Printer size paper (ideally waxed paper)
- Pen
- Ruler
- Scissors
- Colored pens
- Tape
- Thick cardstock
- Adhesive putty

1 Fold the paper in half, top to bottom. Then fold it left to right and unfold again to leave a central crease.

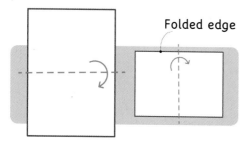

Folded edge

2 Turn down the top corners so they meet at the central crease. Turn up the bottom sections, one to the front and one to the back. Tuck the ends over so you have a triangle shape.

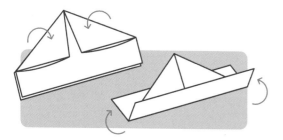

3 Push ends A and B toward each other, making a diamond shape.

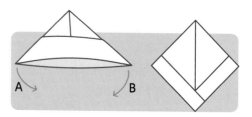

A   B

4 Fold the bottom corner up to meet the top corner. Repeat on the other side, making a triangle shape.

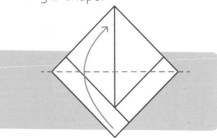

5 Push corners C and D down to meet each other, making another diamond. Pull tips E and F apart, and a boat will magically appear!

E   F

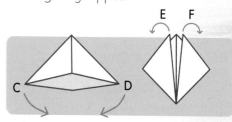

C   D

6 To make the keel, which gives a boat stability, cut this shape from thick cardstock. Cover it with tape to make it waterproof. Push the wide end up into the fold on the bottom of the boat and attach it with tape.

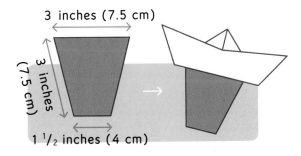

3 inches (7.5 cm)

3 inches (7.5 cm)

1 1/2 inches (4 cm)

7 Decorate your boat. If you did not use waxed paper, waterproof the sides by covering them with tape. Launch your boat!

The Science:
DRAG AND STREAMLINING

Compare how your boats sail. As a boat moves through water, a rubbing force called **friction** slows it down. This is the same force that heats your hands when you rub them. In water or air, this force is called **drag**. The paper boat is more streamlined than the bottle boat—its pointed front allows water to pass more easily along its sides, and this reduces drag.

Your boat floats best with small weights aboard. If it leans to one side, try to balance it by placing a blob of adhesive putty on the other side.

MAKE A PARACHUTE

Do heights make your legs go wobbly?
Now you can make and test a parachute
WITHOUT plunging from a plane!

1 Fold a plastic garbage bag into quarters. Draw a curve above the corner where both folds join, as shown.

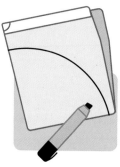

2 Ask an adult to cut along the curve through all four layers of plastic. This will give you two large plastic circles. Discard one of them.

ASK AN ADULT

DID YOU KNOW?

Air resistance stops a human
from falling faster than about
125 miles (200 km) per hour.
This is called terminal velocity.

3 Take your plastic circle and fold eight sticky labels over the outer edge, an equal distance apart. Punch a hole through each label.

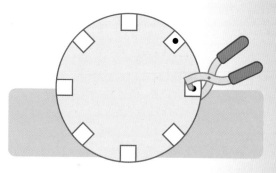

4 Measure and cut eight 6-foot (180 cm) lengths of string.

5 Fold one of the lengths of string in half. Push the looped end through one of the holes from underneath, thread the two ends through the loop, then pull them tight. Repeat for the other seven holes.

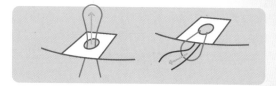

You will need...

- Plastic garbage bag
- Marker
- Scissors
- Sticky labels
- Hole puncher
- Tape measure
- String
- Curtain ring, paperclip, or small toy

6 Gather the strings together so their ends are level and tie them in one big knot to the curtain ring, or you could try using a small toy. Your parachute is ready to test out!

If you don't have a hole puncher, you can make the holes using a sharp pencil.

The Science: GRAVITY AND DRAG

The force of gravity pulls any object with **mass** toward the Earth. As the parachute falls, its large surface area traps trillions of air **molecules**, which push back and produce drag. This is called air resistance. It makes the parachute fall at a slow and steady terminal velocity.

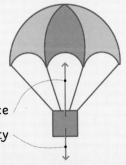

Air resistance

Gravity

KITE FLIGHT

Take creative science to new heights with this simple kite design. Then watch your kite catch the breeze and soar up into the sky!

WARNING!
DON'T fly your kite alone or in thundery weather. NEVER fly it near busy roads, trees, buildings, and especially nowhere near power lines.

3 To make the struts, stick two pencils together end to end using duct tape. Repeat for the other two pairs of pencils. Tape the struts to the kite, as shown. Wrap a piece of duct tape around corners A and B.

1 Take a large plastic sheet and draw on this kite shape, starting with the rectangle. Cut the shape out.

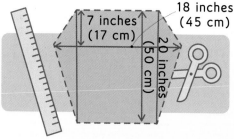

18 inches
(45 cm)

7 inches
(17 cm)

20 inches
(50 cm)

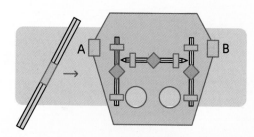

A

B

2 Use small scissors to cut out two 3 ½-inch (9-cm) wide circles. The center of each circle should be 5 inches (12 cm) from the bottom edge.

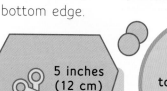

5 inches
(12 cm)

It may help to draw around a circular object.

4 Ask an adult to make a hole through the duct tape on corners A and B using a sharp pencil. Cut a 33-inch (85 cm) length of string and tie the ends securely to the holes.

ASK AN ADULT

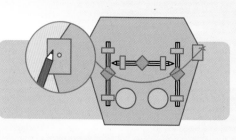

14

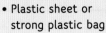

You will need...

- Plastic sheet or strong plastic bag
- Pen
- Ruler
- Large scissors
- Small scissors
- Duct tape

- 6 pencils for struts
- Metal ring or paperclip
- Sharp pencil
- Strong string or twine

The Science: LIFT

The wind pushes on the kite, but the string stops it from moving away. Instead the string makes the kite tilt at an angle to the wind and pushes the air downward. This produces an upward force called **lift**, which raises the kite in the air. By pulling the kite toward you, you can increase this force and raise the kite higher.

Instead of pairs of pencils, you could use wooden dowels for the struts.

5 Make a loop in the string and push it through a metal ring. Bend the loop back, slide the ring down a little, and turn it over bottom to top, then pull tight.

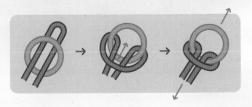

6 Cut a 66-foot (20 m) length of string and tie one end to the metal ring. Take your kite outside on a windy day. Stand with your back to the wind, hold the kite high, and let it go, but keep hold of the string! With luck your kite will fly high!

FLYING DISK

Put science in a spin with your very own flying disk...

1 Roll five ½-inch (1.2-cm) wide blobs of adhesive putty. Stick four of them onto the rim of a plastic plate an equal distance apart. Put the fifth blob in the center.

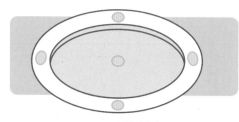

2 Press the second plate onto the first one, taking care not to break the rims.

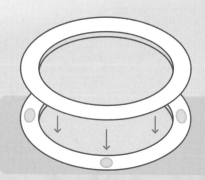

3 Tape the rims tightly together.

You will need...

- Two light plastic plates (at least 8 inches/20 cm diameter)
- Adhesive putty
- Tape
- Pens to decorate

4 Try out your flying disk on a windless day. Stand side-on to the direction you want to throw the disk, hold it level, quickly move it forward, and release it with a backwards flick of the wrist.

You could decorate your flying disk using colored pens.

Flying disk challenge

Which throw makes the flying disk go farthest?
a) Disk held level with spin
b) Disk tilted downward
c) Disk tilted upward
d) Disk held level but no spin

Answer:
a) Can you explain your results in terms of lift and angular momentum (see The Science?)

The Science: BERNOULLI PRINCIPLE AND ANGULAR MOMENTUM

Your flying disk flies well for two reasons. First, its shape produces lift, which keeps it in the air. Here's what happens:

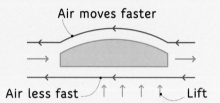

Air moves faster

Air less fast ↑ ↑ ↑ ↑ Lift

The Bernoulli Principle states that when a gas or fluid speeds up, its pressure drops. Since air moves faster over the disk's upper surface, the **air pressure** is higher on the lower surface. The difference in air pressure produces lift.

The second reason your flying disk flies so well is because spin keeps it stable in the air. The steady spin is due to a quality called **angular momentum**. The more mass and the faster the disk spins, the greater its angular momentum. The adhesive putty inside your flying disk increases its mass and boosts its angular momentum, making it fly better.

SNOWBALL FLIGHT TESTS

Try out these wet and dry snowballs to see which flies farthest. Who says scientists don't have fun?

1 Bundle together a handful of cotton balls to make a snowball. Now make a second snowball the same size as the first one—use a ruler to check they are the same size.

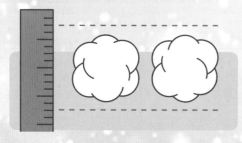

2 Put one ball under a faucet until it is damp but not soaking wet.

3 Wrap both balls in plastic wrap.

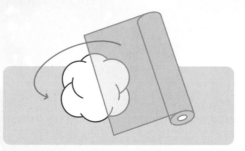

4 Throw each ball in the same direction with the same force. Which goes farthest?

You may like to throw the balls at a friend and invite them to throw them back!

You will need...

- Cotton balls
- Ruler
- Water
- Plastic wrap

If it's snowy, try this experiment with real snow! The best snow for snowballs is slightly damp, so look for snow that has the sun on it or is near a building. It will refreeze when you make it into a snowball. To give one ball more mass, pack more snow into it, but take care to make both your snowballs the same size.

The Science: DRAG, MASS, AND MOMENTUM

As the balls fly through the air, the air resistance (drag) slows them down. Eventually gravity pulls the snowballs back down to Earth. The damp ball has more mass than the dry ball, which means the damp ball has more **momentum**. Drag takes longer to slow it down, so it travels farther.

This is a comparison experiment. Two objects—in this case balls—are exactly the same apart from one change, so any difference in what happens to the objects must be due to this change. In a comparison experiment, the object that isn't changed is called the control.

WHAT GOES AROUND COMES APART

Before we get mixing, let's try separating substances. It's as easy as spinning a wheel!

1 Quarter-fill a ½-ounce (15-ml) bottle with olive oil. Fill the rest of the bottle with white vinegar.

2 Pour the mixture into a bowl. Add one-third of a teaspoon of smooth mustard. Stir until the mustard has disappeared. Put the mixture back into the bottle and screw on the lid.

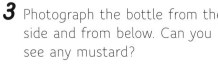

3 Photograph the bottle from the side and from below. Can you see any mustard?

4 **ASK AN ADULT** Ask an adult to help you tape the bottle firmly to two of the spokes on the back wheel of a bicycle.

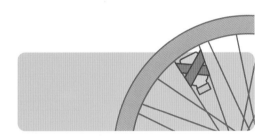

5 **ASK AN ADULT** Ask an adult to put on goggles and gloves. They should set the bike to a high gear, turn it upside down, and turn one of the pedals as fast as they can for one minute, then stop the wheel using the brakes.

You will need...

- Clean ½-ounce (15-ml) screw-top plastic bottle
- Olive oil
- White vinegar
- Bowl
- Smooth mustard
- Teaspoon
- Camera
- Bicycle
- Duct tape or strong packing tape
- Scissors
- Goggles
- Thick gloves

DID YOU KNOW?

A centrifuge machine separates mixtures by spinning. Medical scientists use them to separate the ingredients of blood.

The Science:
CENTRIPETAL, CENTRIFUGAL

Olive oil is lighter than vinegar, so it floats, but mustard stops olive oil from forming a floating layer. When you add mustard, the mixture stays mixed up.

As you spin the mixture, it tries to fly off in a straight line. This is called **centrifugal effect**. But the wheel rim provides a **centripetal force** that pushes the mixture toward the center of the wheel. Centrifugal effect depends on an object's mass: the greater the mass, the bigger the effect. Since the molecules in mustard and vinegar are more massive than in olive oil, they are pushed harder toward the wheel and the mixture separates.

6 Cut the duct tape and remove the bottle. Now compare the mixture with your photographs from step 3. Can you see olive oil at the top of the mixture and mustard at the bottom?

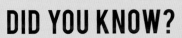

MAKE GIANT BUBBLES

When bubbles get super-sized, so does the fun! Here's how to make big bubbles, and EVEN BIGGER bubbles!

1 Put 7 ounces (200 ml) of hot tap water into a 16.9-ounce (500-ml) screw-top bottle. Add 1 ½ tablespoons of glycerine and enough dishwashing liquid to fill the bottle to the brim.

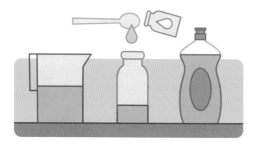

2 Screw the lid on tight and shake the bottle for 20 seconds. Then leave it for at least 3 days. Cool the mixture in the fridge for at least one hour.

3 Cut a plastic drinking straw in half. Thread a 24-inch (60-cm) length of string through both pieces of straw and knot the string. This is your smaller bubble wand.

4 For even bigger bubbles, cut two pieces of string, 39 inches (1 m) and 47 inches (1.2 m) long. Tie the ends of the shorter string to the ends of two long sticks. Tie the longer string to the first string, as shown.

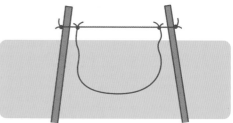

5 Pour the bubble mixture into a large bowl. Take your smaller wand and, holding the straws together, dip it into the mixture until the string is soaked. Open the straws and sweep the bubble wand around to release a bubble. Now try this with the larger wands!

DID YOU KNOW?

In 2006 Sam Heath blew a giant bubble around 19 boys and girls!

You will need...

- Measuring jug
- Water
- 16.9-ounce (500-ml) screw-top bottle
- Tablespoon
- Glycerine
- Dishwashing liquid
- Plastic drinking straw
- Scissors
- Thin string
- Tape measure
- Two long sticks
- Large bowl

The Science:
BUBBLE WALLS AND EVAPORATION

As you separate the wands, a thin film of detergent and water forms between the strings. The air makes this film bulge. As you move the wands, the film snaps around the air to make a bubble; it squeezes the bubble into the smallest area it can, which is always a sphere. The bubble wall is like a water and detergent sandwich.

Detergent ⟶ ⟵ Water

When some of the water molecules **evaporate**, the wall weakens and pops. Glycerine thickens the detergent layers, so the water can't evaporate as easily. Becasue the bubbles have stronger walls, you can blow bigger, longer-lasting bubbles. Cool bubbles don't burst as easily either. This is because water evaporates less quickly in cooler air.

This experiment works best on a windless day.

VOLCANIC ERUPTIONS

Imagine a volcano erupting in your garden! This one oozes masses of red lava. Then turn the page for an explosive eruption!

 MESS WARNING! Food coloring stains! Wear old clothes and set up the experiment on bare earth.

1 Put a small pot, open end down, in the bottom of a bucket. Press sand into the bucket. If the sand is dry, sprinkle on a little water.

2 Turn out a sandcastle.

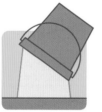

3 Measure out 13.5 ounces (400 ml) of vinegar. Add enough red food coloring to make a strong red color.

4 Measure out ½ cup (130 g) of baking soda. Press sand onto the inside of the pot at the top of your sandcastle to hide it. Pour the baking soda into the pot.

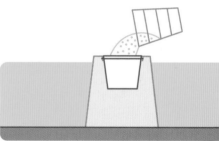

ICE VOLCANO

If you don't have sand, use ice! Put a small pot, open end down, in a bucket. Put a plastic bag in the bucket, tucking it around the pot, and fill with water. Freeze for 24 hours. Take the bag out of the bucket and peel it off the ice. Follow steps 3 to 5, putting the baking soda into the hollow in the ice left by the pot.

Always wear gloves when handling ice.

toy bucket

thin plastic bag

pot, open end down

You will need...

- Small pot
- Kid's beach bucket
- Sand
- Water
- 13.5 ounces (400 ml) white vinegar or lemon juice
- Measuring cup
- Red food coloring
- ½ cup (130 g) baking soda
- Kitchen scales

5 Trickle the colored vinegar onto the baking soda and watch as red lava erupts and oozes down the volcano!

The Science:
CHEMICAL REACTIONS: ACIDS AND BASES

You made your volcano erupt by mixing vinegar with baking soda. Vinegar contains an acid; it's at least 4% acetic acid. Baking soda is a base. When mixed with water, both of these chemicals can dissolve other substances, but they aren't strong enough to harm humans! You do notice the acid if you put vinegar on your tongue. The acid makes vinegar taste sour.

When you combined the acid and the base, you created new molecules in what scientists call a **chemical reaction**. The acid and base combined to make water, a salt called sodium ethanoate, and carbon dioxide gas. It's the gas bubbles that make the lava fizz and expand until it flows down the volcano.

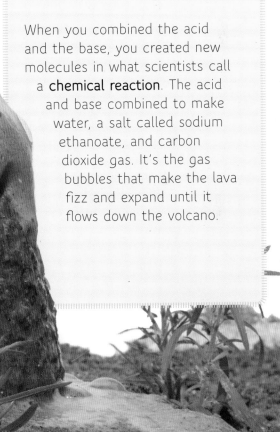

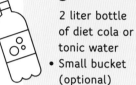

You will need...

- 2 liter bottle of diet cola or tonic water
- Small bucket (optional)

Packet of mints (the type with a hole in the middle!)

This explosive volcano shoots cola lava high into the air. It's fast and furious, and only lasts a few seconds!

1 Place the cola in a warm place for at least two hours.

2 Unwrap the mints and get four of them ready.

3 Stand the bottle outside, away from buildings—you can put it in a bucket for stability. Open the bottle very slowly. Try not to let too much gas escape.

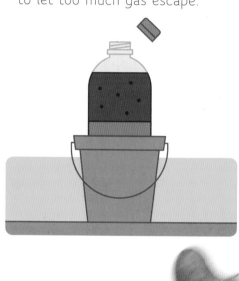

MESS WARNING!
The sticky cola goes everywhere! Wash it away with water.

If you use less than 2 liters of cola, drop in only two mints.

4 As soon as you've taken off the cap, drop four mints into the bottle and quickly step back. The cola lava will shoot high up into the air!

The Science: BUBBLES, SURFACES, AND REAL VOLCANOES

Unlike the previous experiment, this eruption isn't a chemical reaction; it's a physical change.

The cola drink contains dissolved carbon dioxide gas. The gas is under pressure in the liquid and can't escape. Warming the bottle boosts this pressure. When you add mints, you provide rough surfaces for gas molecules to stick to. The molecules form bubbles. Now they can escape! They rise to the surface very fast, and the escaping gas shoots liquid from the bottle.

Some real volcanoes produce gentle streams of lava. But if there's a lot of gas in the lava, the eruptions can be explosive, just like this one!

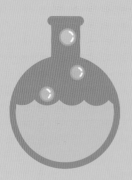

SOIL SECRETS

Soil makes a wonderful, muddy mess, but what is it made of and how does it compare to sand? Let's take a close look!

WARNING!
Soil contains bacteria. Put a bandage on any cuts and wear gloves!

1 Weigh out 3 ½ ounces (100 g) of soil and put it in a saucer.

2 Put 3 ½ ounces (100 g) of sand in a separate saucer.

3 Use a magnifying glass to examine the soil and the sand. What do you see? How are the soil and sand different?

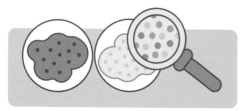

4 Put a coffee filter in a funnel and put the funnel on a jar.

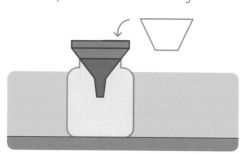

5 Put the soil into the filter paper. Little by little, pour 3 ½ ounces (100 ml) of water over the soil, allowing it to soak through before adding more. Wait five minutes, then measure the height of the water in the jar.

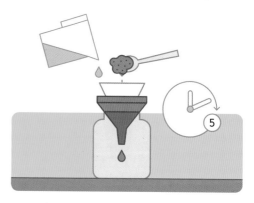

6 Empty the jar and repeat steps 4–5 using sand. Which let the most water through: soil or sand?

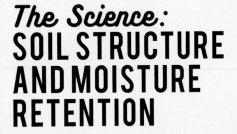

You will need...

- Gloves
- 2 small saucers
- Old tablespoon
- Kitchen scales
- Soil
- Sand
- Magnifying glass
- 2 coffee filter papers
- Large funnel
- Glass jar
- Water
- Measuring cup
- Ruler

The Science: SOIL STRUCTURE AND MOISTURE RETENTION

Like the snowball activity on pages 18-19, this is a comparison experiment. The aim was to discover which sample retained most moisture.

At step 3, you saw that sand is made of grains (tiny stones), while soil consists of crumbs made of smaller grains stuck together. When you poured water over the sand, the water slipped between the stones and nearly all of it ended up in the jar. But when you poured water on the soil, the water soaked into the crumbs and coated the tiny soil grains. Far less water reached the jar. Soil is like a sponge: it soaks up water and stays moist, even in dry weather.

Soil challenge

1) Why do plants grow better in soil than in sand?
2) What would happen to plants and animals if there were no soil?

Answers:
1) Soil retains water, and plants need water to survive.
2) Plants would die, and without plants to eat most animals would starve.

29

GROW POTATOES

Did you know you can grow a potato plant from a potato? Here's how to do it!

WARNING!
Soil contains bacteria.
Put a bandage on any
cuts on your hands,
and wear gloves!

1 Wash and dry a potato and leave it in a dark place for a few days until its "eyes" start to sprout. Ask an adult to cut the potato in half as shown.

ASK AN ADULT

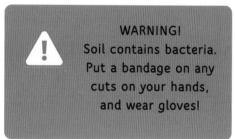

2 Push 4 toothpicks into one half of the potato, halfway up the sides.

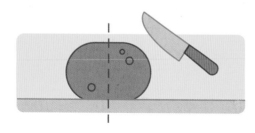

3 Fill a jar with water. Rest the toothpicks on the rim so that the cut side of the potato is underwater. Put the jar in a light place.

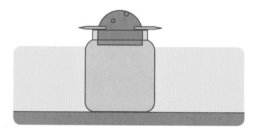

4 Keep the water topped up. After a few days, roots and shoots will appear.

5 Put 1-2 inches (2.5-5 cm) of small stones into a clean plant pot. Add potting compost to fill one third of the pot. Put the potato on it, cut side down. Cover it with about 3 inches (7.5 cm) of potting compost.

You will need...

- Gloves
- Potato
- Knife
- Toothpicks
- Glass jar
- Water
- Plant pot
- Small stones
- Potting compost or garden soil

The best potatoes to use are seed potatoes from a garden center or organic potatoes.

6 Water the compost until it is moist but not soggy. In a few days, the shoots will push up through the compost. Keep adding more compost until the pot is full. After several months, your potato plant should produce potatoes!

Choose a potato with lots of "eyes" —these are buds that will sprout new shoots.

The Science:
VEGETATIVE REPRODUCTION

Everyone knows that new plants grow from seeds. But new plants can also grow from bits of old plants, without seeds or flowers. This is called vegetative reproduction. The new plants are copies of the original plant. Some simple animals can grow new parts too, but complex animals, such as humans, cannot. If they could, scientists could grow new humans from body bits!

A potato is a tuber—a living structure produced in the roots. It is rich in a substance called starch. The shoots of the potato plant grow using food energy in the starch.

GROWING CUTTINGS

Here's how to turn one pretty plant into lots of plants! This experiment is best done in spring or summer, when plants are growing.

1 **ASK AN ADULT** Ask an adult to cut the top 3–4 inches (7.5–10 cm) from a growing shoot, just below a leaf. The shoot should be young and green, not old and woody.

2 Remove any leaves from the bottom 1 inch (2.5 cm) of the cutting, and put it in a jar with 1 inch (2.5 cm) of water. Keep the water topped up, and after 3 to 4 weeks, roots will appear. When the roots are 2 inches (5 cm) long, the cutting is ready to plant.

3 Put some small stones in a flowerpot. Wearing gloves, fill the pot with compost to about ½ inch (1.2 cm) below the rim.

4 Make a hole in the compost with a pencil and stand the cutting in the hole. Gently pack compost around the roots.

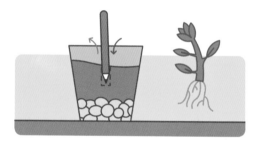

5 Stand the pot on a saucer. Add water to the pot, up to the brim.

6 Cover the pot and cutting with a plastic bag secured with a rubber band. Remove the bag after a few days and keep your new plant's compost moist.

You will need...

- Leafy plant
- Scissors
- Jar
- Warm water
- Trowel
- Potting compost or soil
- Gloves
- Small stones
- Flowerpot and saucer
- Ruler
- Pencil or stick
- Clear plastic bag
- Rubber band or string

Not all plants will grow from a cutting, and not all cuttings will grow, so try 2 or 3 cuttings. Good plants to use are coleuses (below) and rosemary.

A baby spider plant grows from the main plant and already has roots. Put one in a shallow tub to grow a cutting more quickly.

The Science:
HOW PLANTS GROW

Your cutting is another example of vegetative reproduction (see page 31). It grows roots to absorb water from the soil. Some water travels to the leaves, where it combines with carbon dioxide gas from the air to make food for the plant using sunlight. This process is called **photosynthesis**. As your cutting grows, it sprouts more leaves to make more food.

Plants do most of their growing at their roots, shoots, and leaves, because these areas are vital for their survival.

GLASS GARDEN

Did you know that you can put plants in a sealed jar and they will keep growing? Here's how to make a glass garden...

WARNING!
Soil contains bacteria. Put a bandage on any cuts on your hands, and wear gloves! DON'T pick wild plants in case they're protected by law or are poisonous.

1 Take a large glass jar with a sealable lid. Wash it in soapy water and dry it well.

2 Ask an adult to help you collect some soil.

ASK AN ADULT

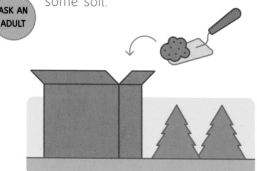

3 Ask an adult to help you dig up some small plants from your yard (or you could buy some from a garden center). Choose a variety of plants to make your garden more interesting (see page 35). Make sure you dig up the roots as well.

ASK AN ADULT

4 Collect a few clumps of moss for your glass garden. Look for it on fallen wood in damp, shady places.

You will need...

- Glass jar (32 to 96 ounces/1 to 3 l)
- Cardboard box
- Trowel
- Gloves
- Soil
- Moss
- Pieces of wood
- Small plants
- Spoon
- Small stones
- Spray bottle
- Water
- Tweezers

PLANT IDEAS

Choose woodland plants that need light, but not direct sunlight. Small, slow-growing plants are best. Flowering plants don't do so well.

- Spider ferns
- Ivy
- Maidenhair fern
- Moss
- Starfish plant
- Nerve plant
- Aquamarine
- Golden clubmoss
- *Helexine* (Baby's Tears)
- "Moon Valley" friendship plant
- Creeping Fig
- *Begonia rex*

5 Find one or two small pieces of fallen wood to make an interesting feature.

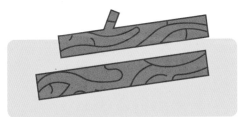

6 Put your jar on its side and spoon in enough small stones to cover the bottom.

35

7 Sprinkle some soil over the stones. Remember to wear gloves.

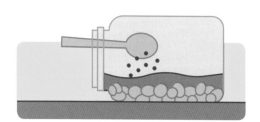

8 Spray your plants and wood with water to dampen them.

The Science:
HOW PLANTS USE WATER AND GASES

Another name for a glass garden is a terrarium. "Terra" means Earth in Latin, and your glass garden works like a mini planet Earth. The soil and plants in the glass garden lose water molecules by evaporation. The water vapor cools and **condenses** on the glass, and water then trickles down into the soil. On Earth, water vapor condenses into clouds and falls as rain. This is known as the water cycle (see page 63).

In your glass garden, just as in the outside world, the plants take in carbon dioxide gas for photosynthesis, and produce oxygen gas, helping to keep a balance of gases in the air.

Water condenses ⋯⋯⋯   Water evaporates

9 Put your wood in the jar, then place your plants on the soil using tweezers. Close the lid and put the jar in a well-lit place, but not in direct sunlight or it will get too hot.

EVERLASTING FLOWERS

Some flowers last only a few days, but by pressing them you can make them last a lifetime. Here's how to do it...

1 Pick a variety of garden flowers—ask an adult first—or buy a bunch of flowers.

ASK AN ADULT

2 Look at the Flower Structures box, then look at your flowers through a magnifying glass. Can you see sepals, petals, stamens, or carpels?

3 Spread a sheet of newspaper on a board and lay your flowers on the newspaper. Put another sheet of newspaper on top of the flowers and weigh it down with a few heavy books.

Make sure the flowers are not touching.

FLOWER STRUCTURES

Flowers come in all shapes and sizes, but they have these structures:

Stamen: a stalk and a blob containing dusty pollen

Ovary: the place where seeds form

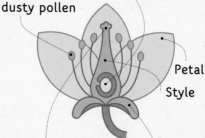

Petal

Style

Stigma: a sticky pad that receives pollen from insects

Sepals: little leaves ringing the base of petals. These are the remains of the flower buds.

Carpel: the structure containing the stigma, style, and ovary

Some flowering plants have many little flowers on a single head.

You will need...

- Fresh flowers
- Magnifying glass
- Old newspapers
- Piece of board
- Heavy books

The Science:
HOW FLOWERS WORK

For flowers to produce seeds, the pollen from the stamens of one flower must be transferred to the carpels of another flower. For most garden flowers, insects do this job. An insect is attracted to a flower by its bright color and scent. When it lands on the flower, pollen sticks to it. The insect then visits another flower and the pollen rubs off on the flower's stigma. The insect is rewarded with a sugary drink called nectar found in the base of the flower. The pollen grows into the ovary and helps to form a seed, which can grow into a new plant.

4 Wait at least four weeks before you remove the flowers; it will take that long for them to dry out.

BARK RUBBING

A tree is a giant plant, but why is it covered in tough stuff? A tree's bark is like its fingerprint! Let's investigate by making bark rubbings.

1 Get your tree detective notebook and pen ready! Now, find a tree with textured bark. Note the location of the tree, what type of tree it is (if you know), and the date.

2 Examine the tree's bark with a magnifying glass. Is anything growing on the bark? Are there any bugs on it? Jot down your findings in your notebook.

3 Gently scratch the bark with the side of a coin, but try not to damage the bark. Give it a sniff! Does it have a strong scent?

4 Take a sheet of paper and hold it against the tree trunk.

5 Hold the side or blunt end of a crayon against the paper and rub. The pattern of the bark should appear.

6 Repeat steps 4 and 5 for a different tree. Use a different color crayon. Compare your bark rubbings.

It's best to lay the paper lengthways against the trunk and rub the crayon up and down. Take care: if you press too lightly, the pattern may not appear. If you press too hard, the paper may tear.

You will need...

- Notebook
- Pen
- Magnifying glass
- Coin
- Printer size white paper
- Wax crayons

The Science: TREE BARK

Bark is the dead outer layers of a tree trunk. It has two vital jobs: first, it helps to hold up the tree and stop it collapsing under its own weight. Secondly, bark keeps out harmful insects, fungi, and bacteria. (As you may have found out, that doesn't stop some bugs and smaller plants from living on bark.) Some trees shed bark to remove harmful pests. Other trees store chemicals in their bark to kill bacteria and stop the bark from rotting.

As a tree grows, its bark stretches and cracks. Each **species** of tree has a different type of bark.

Tree trunk challenge

This is a challenge for yourself and a friend. Select a number of trees and compare their bark. Ask your friend to close their eyes and turn around three times. With their eyes still closed, lead them to a tree. Can your friend identify the tree by touching its bark? Now swap places with your friend and see how well you do.

41

SNAIL RACING

Welcome to the world's s-l-o-w-e-s-t sport.
On your marks, get set, and...SQUIRM!

1 Ask an adult to make some holes in the lid of a plastic pot. Put some lettuce leaves in the pot.

ASK AN ADULT

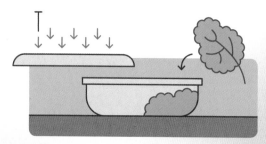

2 Find two snails; they often hide in dark, damp places. Put them in the pot and put the lid on. Place the pot in a dark place for 20 to 30 minutes.

3 Fill a bucket with water and pour it over some paving stones to wet them—but don't flood the place!

4 Place two small stones about 39 inches (1 m) apart on the paving stones.

5 Place a snail next to each stone. Give them 10-15 minutes to get moving. Study them with a magnifying glass. Can you see how they move? Can you see the main parts of their bodies?

This activity works best at dusk on a damp evening.

You will need...

- Nail or other pointed object
- Clean plastic pot with lid
- Lettuce leaves
- Two snails

- Bucket
- Water
- Two small stones
- Tape measure
- Magnifying glass
- Watch

If you don't have a tape measure, you can mark a length of string at 2-inch (5-cm) intervals and use that instead.

6 Measure the distance that each snail travels from its starting stone in 30 minutes. The winner is the snail that travels farthest!

7 After the race, return the snails to the places you found them.

DID YOU KNOW?

In 1995 Archie the snail moved 13 inches (33 cm) in two minutes. It was the world's fastest snail.

The Science:
SNAIL MOVEMENT

Snails belong to a group of animals called mollusks. Most mollusks live in the sea. Garden snails live on land, but they do like damp conditions, which is why you put water on their racetrack.

Unlike us, snails don't have legs. A wave of squeezing muscle movement passes along the foot and the snail moves forward on a trail of slime.

Shell

Tentacles with eyes

Head

Foot

Body

GIANT SPIDER'S WEB

Are you brave enough to discover scary spider secrets? Find out as you weave your very own giant web!

1 Find a spot where you can attach your web at eight points (see circle opposite). Each anchor point should be at least 39 inches (1 m) from the next one.

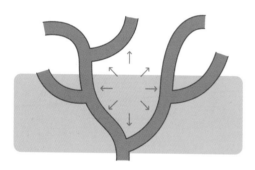

2 Cut a length of string about 47 inches (1.2 m) long.

3 Tie or pin one end of the string to an anchor point. Pull it across to the opposite point and attach it in place. Mark the center point of the string.

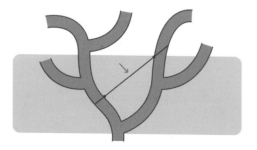

4 Repeat steps 2 and 3, but twist the new string around the center point before you attach the loose end to its anchor point. Repeat with two more strings, keeping them taut. These are called radial threads.

5 Repeat step 2. This time tie the string about halfway along a radial thread and take it around toward the central point in a spiral. Each time you cross a radial string, wrap the string you are holding around it. Try to keep the strings tight.

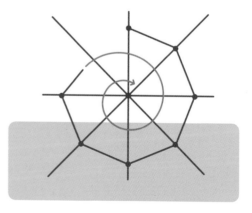

6 Trim any untidy ends with scissors. As a finishing touch, tie a toy spider to the web!

You will need...

- Ball of string
- Scissors
- Tape measure
- Push pins
- Pen
- Toy or paper spider

The Science: SPIDER WEBS

Congratulations! You've spun a web just like a real spider. Spiders start with the radial threads and then add spiral threads. The spiral threads are sticky and keep the radial threads taut. Although spider silk is very light, it is strong enough to hold insects caught on the sticky threads. Spiders also use silk for wrapping up victims and making nests.

You could attach your web to a doorway or fence using push pins. Or try tying the strings to a garden arch or tree branches. If a string breaks, just tie the ends together and keep going.

DID YOU KNOW?

Some spiders use silk threads to fly far through the air, blown by the wind.

BIRD BREAKFAST

Make a bird feeder to help make life easier for wild birds. Then turn the page to find a delicious bird breakfast recipe...

The best time to do this project is in the winter, when birds are hungry. Don't try it in the spring when birds are feeding their chicks. The growing chicks need insects and worms rather than the food you put out.

1 Take a box and draw a cutting line around it 1 ½ inches (4 cm) from the bottom. Cut off and discard the top of the box.

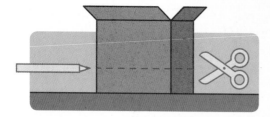

2 Ask an adult to make a hole in each side of the box using a push pin and the ends of a pair of scissors.

ASK AN ADULT

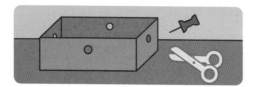

3 Cut two 24-inch (60-cm) lengths of string. Thread one of them through one of the holes from the outside; it may help to push it through the hole with the point of a pencil. Knot the end around the string, as shown.

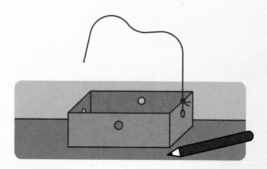

4 Thread the other end of the string through the opposite hole from the outside, and tie it to the string.

5 Take the other length of string, thread it through the two unused holes, and tie the ends as before. Add some bird seed to the feeder.

You will need...

- Box or carton (34 ounces/1 liter)
- Pen
- Ruler
- Scissors
- Push pin
- String
- Pencil
- Bird seed

DID YOU KNOW?

Small birds need to eat 25-50% of their body weight in seeds every day just to survive.

The best place to hang the bird feeder is from a thin branch that cats can't get to. Choose a branch that you can see from a window so you can watch the birds from indoors using binoculars.

6 Ask an adult to hang the feeder from a thin branch.

ASK AN ADULT

The Science: BIRD FEEDING

Birds need high-energy food because they use so much energy flying and keeping warm. Normally they'll seek out seeds or insects and worms, but these foods are scarce in winter and they'll be happy to eat your food. Seeds are a high-energy food and are ideal for many adult birds.

Hang this bird food next to your bird feeder to attract even more visiting birds!

You will need...

- Plastic cup
- Scissors
- String
- Tape measure
- Bread
- Grater
- Bowl
- Heatproof bowl
- Tablespoon

- Lard, suet, or goose fat
- Microwave oven
- Oats
- Finely chopped nuts
- Pumpkin or sunflower seeds
- Dessert spoon
- Teaspoon

1 Ask an adult to make a hole in the bottom of a plastic cup using scissors, as shown.

ASK AN ADULT

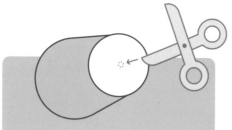

2 Cut a 24-inch (60-cm) length of string. Thread one end through the hole and tie the other end to a short stick. Leave the stick dangling outside the cup.

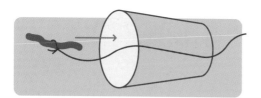

3 Grate half a slice of stale bread into a bowl. Use scissors to snip any large lumps into smaller pieces.

⚠ **WARNING!**
Melted lard is VERY HOT.

4 Add 2 tablespoons of lard to a heatproof bowl. Ask an adult to microwave the lard for about 30 seconds.

ASK AN ADULT

5 Ask an adult to remove the bowl of lard from the microwave. Stir in the breadcrumbs and one tablespoon of oats. Stir in a dessert spoon each of nuts and seeds. The mixture should be dry and greasy. If it is too runny, stir in some more oats.

ASK AN ADULT

6 Scoop the mixture into the cup and press it down. Pull the string so the stick sits on top of the mixture.

Birdwatch challenge:

Using a pair of binoculars and a bird identification book, can you identify which species of birds are visiting? Which birds prefer which food? Sometimes birds squabble over food. Which birds win these contests?

7 Leave the cup in the fridge for three hours or until the mixture is hard. Turn the cup upside-down and press the base of the cup. If the mixture doesn't slide out, ask an adult to cut open the cup.

ASK AN ADULT

8 Tie the bird cake's string to a branch near your bird feeder.

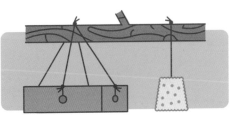

MAKE A WINDSOCK

You can feel it but you never see it. It's always around, but it never stays still. Where does wind come from? Here's one way to find out!

1 *ASK AN ADULT* Ask an adult to cut a 1-inch (2.5-cm) wide ring from the center of a 2 liter plastic bottle. The edges of the ring should be as smooth and straight as possible.

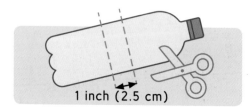

1 inch (2.5 cm)

2 *ASK AN ADULT* Ask an adult to press and flatten the ring, and then make two holes on opposite sides; they could do this with scissor points or a hole puncher.

3 Cut a 16-inch (40-cm) length of string and thread it through the holes. Tie the ends together to make a loop.

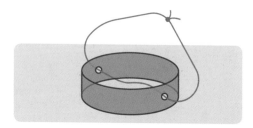

4 Use a ruler and marker to draw 12 to 15 thin strips on a plastic bag, about ¾ inch (2 cm) wide and 20 inches (50 cm) long. Cut them out.

5 Hang the loop up and drape one of the plastic strips over the ring. Tie the strip so the knot is on the ring's bottom edge.

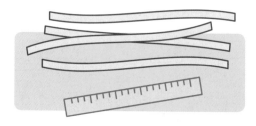

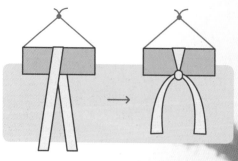

6 Repeat step 5 with the rest of the strips. Try to space them evenly around the ring.

You will need...

- 2 liter plastic bottle
- Small scissors
- Hole puncher
- String
- Plastic bag, such as a garbage bag
- Marker
- Ruler
- Compass

The Science:
WIND AND AIR PRESSURE

Wind is caused by differences in air pressure. Air only moves from areas with high air pressure to places with lower air pressure. In areas of high pressure, cooler air spirals toward the ground. In areas of low pressure, warmer air near the ground spirals upward.

7 Hang your windsock where it will catch the wind. The strips will blow out like streamers, showing which direction the wind is blowing. The stronger the wind, the more it will blow sideways.

Wind diary challenge:

Keep a wind diary for a week. Check your windsock every morning and evening and note whether the wind is zero, light, medium, or strong. Use a compass to find out which direction the wind is blowing from.

MEASURE THE SUN

The Sun is 93 million miles (150 million km) away. But did you know you can measure the Sun's diameter from outdoors?

> **WARNING!**
> NEVER look directly at the Sun. The bright light can damage your eyes.

1 Use a ruler and pencil to draw two parallel lines across a sheet of paper. The lines should be exactly $\frac{1}{10}$ inch (2.5 mm) apart.

Make sure the pencil is sharp

2 Cut a 4 x 6 inches (10 x 15 cm) piece of cardstock. Cut a 1 inch (2.5 cm) square in the cardstock and tape a piece of aluminum foil over the square. Use a push pin to make a hole in the foil.

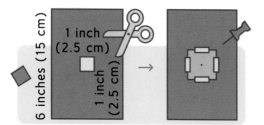

6 inches (15 cm)

1 inch (2.5 cm)

1 inch (2.5 cm)

4 inches (10 cm)

3 Turn the cardstock over and fold down a 1 inch (2.5 cm) flap. Tape the cardstock to the ruler so it lines up with the 10 ¾ inch (27.5 cm) mark.

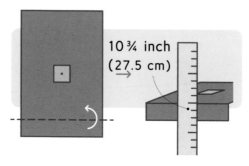

10 ¾ inch (27.5 cm)

4 On a sunny day, put the paper on a table outdoors. The paper should be level with the zero mark on the ruler. Position the card so that its shadow falls on the paper. Move the paper until you see a small, bright circle between the parallel lines. This is an image of the Sun made by sunlight shining through the pinhole.

5 Do these sums to figure out the diameter of the Sun:

For miles: 10.75 ÷ 0.1 = A
 93,000,000 ÷ A = ?

For km: 27.5 ÷ 0.25 = A
 149,600,000 ÷ A = ?

You will need...

- Ruler
- Paper
- Sharp pencil
- Cardstock
- Scissors
- Aluminum foil
- Tape
- Pin
- Calculator
- Pencil

The Science: THE DIAMETER OF THE SUN

The aim of the experiment was to measure the diameter of the Sun. You did it by projecting an image of the Sun through the hole and onto the paper. The image was $\frac{1}{10}$ inch (2.5 mm) across at a distance of 10.75 inches (27.5 cm). Figure A in your sum was the number of times that $\frac{1}{10}$ inch (2.5 mm) could fit into the distance. Next you divided the real distance to the Sun by figure A to give the diameter of the Sun. Scientists have measured the diameter of the Sun as 864,800 miles (1,391,000 km). Your equipment isn't accurate enough to produce this exact figure, but hopefully you got close!

SHADOW SECRETS

Try this experiment and the one on the next page to find some surprising science secrets lurking in the shadows.

1 Cut a circle of thick cardstock 1 inch (2.5 cm) across. Stick it to the end of a pencil with adhesive putty.

Just for fun, you could decorate the circle to look like a UFO!

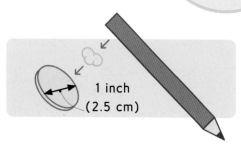

1 inch
(2.5 cm)

2 At midday on a sunny day, put a sheet of paper on a flat surface. Hold the pencil 6 inches (15 cm) above the paper—check the distance with a ruler. Make sure the cardstock circle is facing up. Use a colored pen to draw around the circle's shadow.

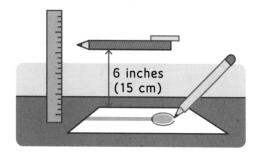

6 inches
(15 cm)

3 Repeat step 2 but hold the cardstock circle 12 inches (30 cm) above the paper. Use a different colored pen to draw around the shadow. Measure and compare the two shadow outlines.

4 Darken a room and switch on the light. Once again, measure the shadows made by the circle at 6 inches (15 cm) and 12 inches (30 cm).

5 Can you explain why the shadows in steps 2 and 3 look different than the shadows in step 4?

You could decorate your paper with a little person running away from the scary UFO's shadow!

You will need...

- Scissors
- Ruler
- Thick cardstock
- Adhesive putty
- Pencil
- Paper
- Two different colored pens

DID YOU KNOW?

When the Moon passes between the Sun and the Earth, the Moon's shadow passes over Earth and it gets dark. This is called a solar eclipse.

The Science:
LIGHT AND SHADOWS

It doesn't matter how far you hold the circle from the paper in sunlight, the shadow always looks the same size. This is because the Sun is very distant, and at midday sunlight hits at right angles. Moving the circle 6 inches (15 cm) nearer the Sun won't block more light, so the shadow stays the same size.

Indoors, things are different. As you raise the circle, its shadow gets bigger and less sharp. It grows because the circle blocks more light as it nears the bulb. At the same time, more light hits the shadow from other angles, making the shadow lighter and more blurred.

This shadow shape-changing experiment works best on a sunny morning or afternoon.

1 Place a 1-inch (2.5-cm) wide ball of adhesive putty on a surface. Stick the pencil and cardstock circle from pages 54-55 into the modeling clay.

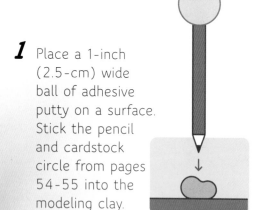

2 Position the pencil so that the circle's shadow falls on the paper. Draw around the shadow in colored pen.

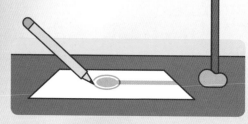

3 Use a protractor to lean the pencil at a 60 degree angle from the surface. Draw around the shadow in a different colored pen.

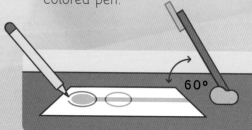

4 Put another sheet of white printer paper on the surface with its edge touching the modeling clay. Bend and flex the paper to make the pencil's shadow wider. Can you make the pencil's shadow bend?

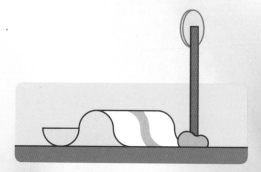

5 Fold the paper on alternate sides to make it corrugated. Each fold should be 1 inch (2.5 cm) apart.

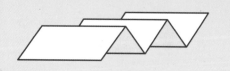

6 Hold the paper up so it forms a staircase with a shadow falling on it. What shape is the shadow?

You should try this experiment around midday.

The Science: SHADOWS AND ANGLES

Your experiment shows how the length and shape of shadows change with the angle between the light and the surface. A shadow lengthens when the Sun sinks, and it also lengthens if the Sun strikes at an angle.

SHADOW TIME

Who needs clocks? All you need is a sunny day and a helpful shadow to tell you the time! Find out how to make a sun clock, or sundial.

1 Use a ruler to draw a right-angled triangle on a piece of cardstock, as shown.

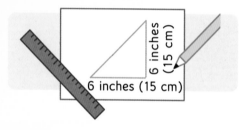

6 inches (15 cm)

6 inches (15 cm)

2 Add a ⁵/₈-inch (1.5-cm) wide rectangle, as shown.

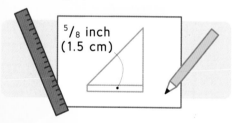

⁵/₈ inch (1.5 cm)

3 Cut out the shape, then cut a concave curve in the side of the triangle. Fold the rectangle over to make a tab.

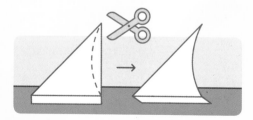

4 Tape the tab to a board so the triangle stands up straight. Use a compass to find north. Point the vertical side of the card triangle toward north. (If you live in the southern hemisphere, point the vertical side to the south.)

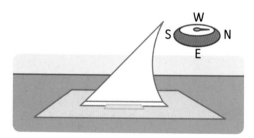

W

S   N

E

DID YOU KNOW?

One of the world's largest sundials is in Jaipur, India. It's nearly 89 feet (27 m) high!

You will need...

- Ruler
- Printer-size sheet of cardstock
- Pencil
- Scissors
- Tape
- Board at least 16 inches (40 cm) square
- Compass

The Science:
THE EARTH AND THE SUN

We get night and day as the Earth spins in space. Our planet takes 24 hours to turn around. When the part of the Earth you are on is facing the Sun, it's day. And when your part of the Earth is facing away from the Sun, it's night.

As the Earth turns, the angle between the Sun and your triangle shape changes, and its shadow moves in a curve. Since the position of the shadow on each hour doesn't change much from day to day, you've created a sun clock, or sundial.

Tomorrow you can use it to tell the time, if it's still sunny!

5 Every hour, put a mark where the tip of the triangle's shadow falls on the board. Write the time next to the mark. At the end of the day, you can join up the marks with a curved line.

● 2:00 pm

Set up this experiment early on a sunny morning. If your sundial leans to one side, you could prop it on each side with a couple of stones.

MAKE A RAINBOW

Why wait for rain? Here are two easy ways to make rainbows!

1 Ask an adult to wash out a spray bottle. Fill it with water.

ASK AN ADULT

2 Stand with your back to the Sun facing a dark surface. Spray water fast and look for rainbows!

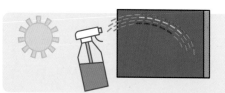

WARNING!
NEVER use a spray bottle that has held chemicals. Ask an adult to wash the bottle. DON'T spray toward eyes. Avoid breathing the spray.

3 Put a sheet of white paper on a clipboard. Use adhesive putty to attach a clear plastic pen tube to the paper.

4 Stand with your back to the Sun. Lean the top of the clipboard toward you and use a magnifying glass to look for rainbow patterns in the shadow under the pen tube.

If you can't see any rainbows at step 4, try a different make of pen tube.

You will need...

- Clean plastic spray bottle
- Water
- White paper
- Clipboard
- Adhesive putty
- Clear plastic pen tube
- Magnifying glass

The Science:
LIGHT AND REFRACTION

Light is a type of electromagnetic radiation. It transfers energy from a source such as the Sun as it travels in waves. The color of the light depends on the **wavelength** of the wave. Sunlight is white; it's a mix of all the colors of light.

As sunlight enters a raindrop, it slows and bends. Because different wavelengths bend at slightly different angles, the colors in sunlight separate and you see a rainbow. Bending light in this way is called refraction. In steps 3 and 4, the sunlight refracts as it passes from air to the plastic.

You can make amazing rainbows by spraying water from a hose (ask permission first). If the hose doesn't have a spray nozzle, just put your thumb over the end.

RAINY DAY SCIENCE

You don't need sun for outdoor science. Rainy days are just as good! Here's how to make a rain gauge.

1 Prepare your seven-day rain diary as shown.

DATE	WATER LEVEL (in.)	INCREASE (in.)

ASK AN ADULT

2 Ask an adult to cut the top third off a 2 liter plastic bottle. It helps to make a small hole before cutting with large scissors. Ask them to trim the cut edge with small scissors.

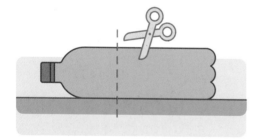

3 If the base of the bottle is uneven, press some modeling clay into the bottom of the bottle to make a flat surface.

4 Remove the cap and turn the top half of the bottle upside down. Place it inside the lower half of the bottle.

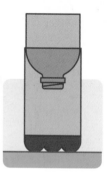

5 Tape the ruler to the lower half of the bottle, making sure it is straight. The zero mark should be level with the top of the modeling clay.

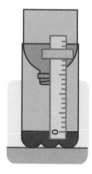

6 Place your rain gauge where rain will fall into it. Wedge bricks or flowerpots around it to stop it from blowing over.

7 Every evening, check the water level in the gauge and write the figure in your diary. If the level has risen, write the difference between the present level and yesterday's level in inches.

- Notebook
- Pencil
- 2-liter clear plastic bottle
- Large scissors
- Small scissors

- Modeling clay or jelly
- Wide tape, ideally clear outdoor tape
- See-through ruler

At step 3, you can use jelly instead of modeling clay to make a really flat surface. Let it set overnight in the bottle.

The Science:
RAIN AND THE WATER CYCLE

We saw a water cycle in the glass garden (page 37): here's how it works. Water molecules evaporate into the air from rivers, lakes, and seas. As air is warmed by the Sun, it rises, only to cool again as it gets higher.

As the air cools, the water molecules condense to form clouds of droplets. If the droplets are heavy enough, they fall as rain. The rain flows back into the rivers, lakes, and seas.

DID YOU KNOW?

In 1966, nearly 71 inches (1.8 m) of rain fell in just 24 hours on the island of Réunion.

MOON MISSION

The Moon is in space, but how far away is it from Earth? Here's how you can see the distance between them in relation to their size!

You'll need an area of paving or path 14 feet (4.4 meters) long. Alternatively you can stick the Earth and Moon to a long wall or fence.

1 Using a compass, draw a 1½-inch (3.8 cm) wide circle on a sheet of paper. This is your Moon. Cut it out and color it gray. You could draw on craters too.

2 On another sheet of paper, draw a 5½-inch (14 cm) wide circle. This is your Earth. Cut it out and color it blue. You could add continents and clouds, too.

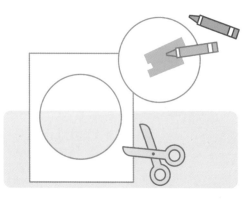

3 Make a stand for your Earth and Moon from cardboard. Make one slightly larger than the other.

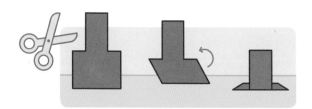

4 Tape the smaller stand to the Moon and the larger one to the Earth.

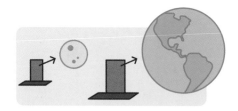

5 Place the Moon at one end of the paved area.

6 Do these sums:
5.5 x 30 = ?
Divide your answer by 12.
The answer is the distance to measure in feet in step 7.

- Compass
- Pencil
- Two sheets of white printer paper
- Crayons, paints, or colored pens
- Ruler
- Scissors
- Cardboard
- Tape
- Calculator
- Tape measure
- Chalk

7 Measure this distance in feet from your Moon and mark the spot with chalk. Put your Earth on the mark.

Shrink the moon challenge:

When the full Moon is near the horizon, roll a tube of paper. Put the tube to one eye and close the other. The Moon seems to shrink!

For unknown reasons, the Moon appears 50 percent larger when you can see other nearer objects. By looking through the tube, you shut out other objects and see the Moon at its real size.

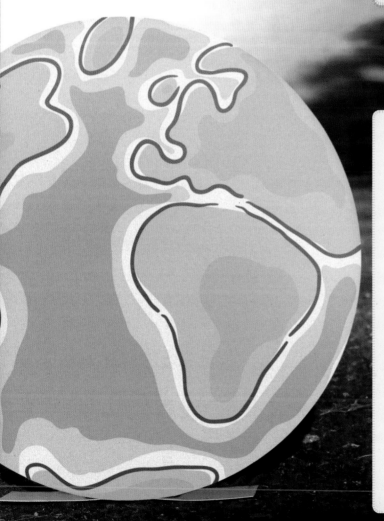

The Science:
THE MOON AND THE EARTH

You've made an accurate plan of the Moon and Earth. The diameter of Earth is about 3.67 times that of the Moon, and the average distance from the Earth to the Moon is about 238,900 miles (384,400 km) —that's 30 times the diameter of Earth. You may be surprised just how small the Moon is compared to Earth and how distant it is. On your plan, the Moon should be 13 feet 9 inches (4.20 m) from your Earth!

MAP THE STARS

Astronomers spend years mapping the stars. You can do it in minutes, and you don't even need a telescope!

FIND A CONSTELLATION

Wait for a clear, moonless night. If you live in the northern hemisphere, see if you can spot the Big Dipper. If you live in the southern hemisphere, look for the Southern Cross.

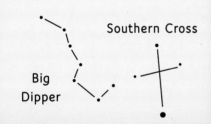

Southern Cross

Big Dipper

2 Wrap a red cloth over the end of a flashlight.

3 Find the **constellation** you're looking for.

4 ASK AN ADULT Ask an adult to hold the flashlight so you can see the cellophane just in front of your face. Look through it at the constellation. Mark the position of each star on the cellophane.

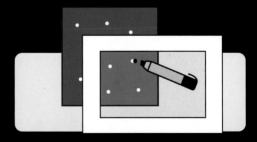

1 To make a frame for your viewer, cut out a rectangle of cardboard. Cut a hole in it and tape some cellophane across the hole. You could decorate the frame.

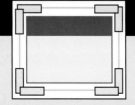

5 Indoors, turn the cellophane over and make felt tip blobs on each of the black blobs you made. Quickly press the felt-tip side on some paper. Lift the cellophane. You've printed a constellation star map! Draw stars over the marks.

You will need...

- Cardboard
- Scissors
- Sheet of cellophane
- Tape
- Small flashlight
- Red cloth
- Black marker
- Water-based felt pens
- White paper

The Science: STARS AND CONSTELLATIONS

Every star, including our Sun, is a giant gas ball. Like our Sun, a star's gravity crushes gas atoms until they fuse together, releasing energy as heat, light, and other types of radiation. Although the stars in a constellation look as if they are all the same distance from us, some are much farther away than others. They're distant from each other in all directions.

If you make a mistake, ask an adult to wipe the marker off the cellophane using white spirit and a kitchen towel.

The final word: OUTDOOR SCIENCE

Science is connected. Everything alive is kept alive by chemical reactions. Animals depend on plants, and plants depend on weather. Animals, the Sun, the Moon, and stars follow the same laws of movement as a flying disk. When you step into the giant science lab of the outdoor world, you're connected too, by knowledge and understanding.

So why not try your own experiments? The FUN is free, the world is waiting. Enjoy!

CHAPTER 6: MAD MIXTURES
BEST EVER BUTTER

This chapter is about mixing materials, but let's start by separating stuff. It's the secret of the best butter ever.

1 Cool the stand mixer bowl in the fridge for two hours.

2 Measure out 1¼-inch (280 ml) of heavy cream and pour it into the cold bowl. Add a pinch of salt if you like salty butter. Switch on the mixer. After about two minutes, the cream will thicken into whipped cream. Keep mixing! The cream will form soft lumps, then turn yellow and look like scrambled egg.

ASK AN ADULT

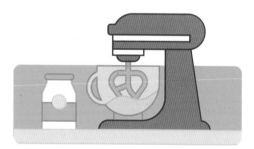

3 If any liquid appears, drain it off. Continue to mix until no more liquid appears.

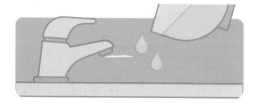

4 Wash your hands, then firmly squeeze the mixture to remove any remaining liquid. Pat the butter dry using tea towels.

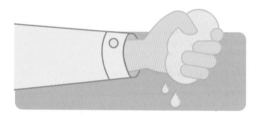

5 Shape the butter using the back of a teaspoon and place it in a container with a cover.

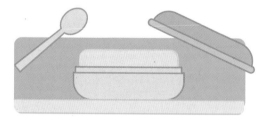

6 Enjoy your homemade butter on toast with your favorite jam. Or use it for the experiments on pages 108, 114 and 116.

You will need...

- Heavy cream
- Measuring cup
- Stand mixer
- Tea towels
- Covered container
- Tablespoon
- Salt (optional)

The Science:
FAT AND PROTEIN

Cream is made from microscopic droplets of fat in water. Each droplet has a thin coat made of **protein**.

Blending breaks open the protein coats. This allows the fat droplets to clump together and form butter. The leftover water and protein is called buttermilk. Some water is left in the butter, making it slightly soft and moist.

Store your butter in the fridge and use it within five days.

SOLID LIQUID WONDERS

Solids are dry and liquids are wet—simple, huh? But some substances can be both wet AND dry. Confused? It's all to do with mixing.

 MESS WARNING! Food coloring stains—wear old clothes!

1 Put two tablespoons of cornstarch into a bowl. Add one tablespoon of water and stir thoroughly.

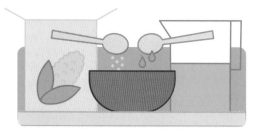

2 Stir in 10 drops of green food coloring. Add a few drops of water and stir again until the mixture is thick and smooth.

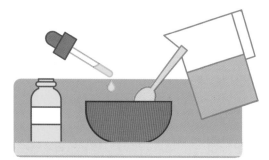

3 Swirl the mixture in the bowl and then run your fingers through it. Now try pressing down on the mixture. What do you notice?

The food coloring isn't vital, but it makes the goo look more interesting—and gross!

You will need...

- Bowl
- Tablespoon
- Water
- Green food coloring
- Cornstarch

The Science:
NON-NEWTONIAN FLUIDS

The mixture flows like a liquid, but when you touch it, WEIRDLY it feels solid. Scientists call this a 'non-Newtonian fluid', after scientist Sir Isaac Newton (1642–1726), who studied the way liquids behave.

The gooey, mixed-up material flows like liquid because it consists of cornstarch grains floating in water. When you press the mixture with your fingers, you push away most of the water, making it feel solid.

The quality that makes a liquid thick or runny is called **viscosity**. A thick liquid is more viscous than a runny liquid because its **molecules** rub together more.

STICKY SITUATIONS

On their own, flour and water aren't sticky, so how can they make glue? *Stick* with this experiment to find out.

MESS WARNING!
This can be quite a messy experiment. Wear old clothes!

1 Cut or tear some newspaper into 30 strips, each measuring about 1 x 8 inches (2.5 x 20 cm).

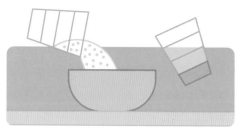

2 Pour some flour into a glass to a height of about 1 inch (2.5 cm), then tip the flour into a bowl. Do the same with of about 1 inch (2.5 cm), of water.

3 Stir the glue mixture until it is thick and creamy, and all the lumps have disappeared.

4 On the printer paper, cover an area 8 x 8 inches (20 x 20 cm) with glue. Lay three strips of newspaper as shown. Gently press the strips with the spoon, so the glue soaks through the newspaper strips.

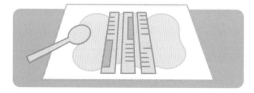

5 Spread some glue on top of the newspaper strips and place three more strips, as shown, pressing down gently.

6 Repeat steps 4 and 5 until you've used up all your strips. Use paper towels to wipe any surplus glue from the edges of the paper. Leave the paper to dry for 24 hours in a warm place.

You will need...

- Newspaper
- Bowl
- Spoon
- Glass
- Ruler
- Scissors
- Sheet of printer-size paper
- Plain flour
- Water
- Paper towels

7 Try and tear the printer paper in half. You should find it is impossible!

The Science: STARCH AND CELLULOSE

Wheat plants use starch to store food. So when wheat seeds are ground up to make flour, the flour contains microscopic grains of starch. The water soaks into the starch grains, which swell and burst, releasing tangled-up starch molecules.

Paper is made of fibers of a substance called cellulose, which is also made by fibers. The starch and cellulose molecules tangle together to make a strong bond that sets hard, so the newspaper will not tear.

DID YOU KNOW?

Sticky starch molecules make sticky rice sticky when you cook it.

73

KITCHEN SUNSET

It's simple to make a sunset in your kitchen.
All you need is a magical milk mixture...

This experiment
should take place
in a darkened room—or
after dark. The glass
should hold at least
2 cups (480 ml)
of water.

3 Place the glass between yourself
and the flashlight so that the light
shines towards you through the
water. Note the color of the mixture.

1 Fill a tall, straight-sided glass with
2 cups (480 ml) of water. Stir in
two tablespoons of milk.

2 Point the
flashlight down
at the surface of
the mixture and
note its color.

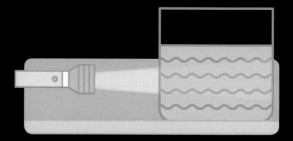

4 Hold the flashlight against the base
of the glass and shine the light up
through the water. Note the color
of the mixture.

DID YOU KNOW?

Sunset and sunrise appear
redder after a volcanic eruption
because particles thrown into
the air reflect away more blue
light than normal.

You will need...

- Measuring cup
- Tall glass or jar with straight sides
- Whole milk
- Small, bright flashlight
- Tablespoon

The Science:
SCATTERING LIGHT

Sunlight contains all the colours of the rainbow. As it shines through Earth's **atmosphere**, it hits trillions of air molecules. At midday, when the sun is overhead and has less atmosphere to travel through, blue light reflects strongly from and between the molecules, so the sky looks blue. At sunset, the sun shines at a low angle and sunlight passes through more of the Earth's atmosphere. Most of the blue light is reflected away, and you see red light, which doesn't reflect strongly from air molecules.

Some sunsets make the sky glow red due to reddish light reflecting off clouds.

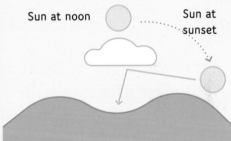

Sun at noon

Sun at sunset

Your experiment works in the same way. Milk molecules reflect blue light more strongly, so the milky water looks bluish from above. But when the light shines *through* the milk, the liquid looks yellower or even reddish, just like a sunset.

GIANT CANDIES

Believe it or not, you can make super-size candies in your own kitchen! Try it for yourself...

1 Put one candy in a glass of water and another on a plate. Put them both in the fridge.

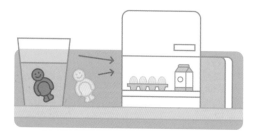

2 After 12 hours, compare the candies. Which candy is bigger? Record their sizes on paper.

DID YOU KNOW?

Gummy candies contain gelatine, which is made from animal protein. It makes them firm and chewy.

3 Add a level dessert spoon of salt to a glass of warm water. Stir the mixture until all the salt has dissolved.

4 Put the biggest candy in the salty water and leave it for two hours. Then measure the size of both candies again. How has the larger candy changed size?

You will need...

- Two gummy candies (like jelly babies or
- gummi bears)
- Glass
- Plate
- Salt
- Water
- Pencil
- Dessert spoon

Wash your hands before you begin this experiment.

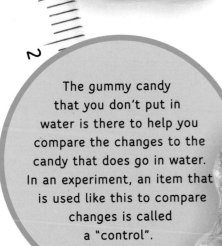

0cm

1

2

5

The gummy candy that you don't put in water is there to help you compare the changes to the candy that does go in water. In an experiment, an item that is used like this to compare changes is called a "control".

The Science: DIFFUSION

Like all liquid or gas molecules, water molecules are constantly moving. Agummy candies contains gelatine, a jelly-like protein molecule. Gelatine has a structure where moving water molecules can squeeze in between the gelatine molecules by a process called diffusion and join with them. The additional water molecules that have joined to the gelatine molecules cause the gummy candies to swell in size and **mass**.

Placing a gummy candy in a salt solution allows salt particles to diffuse into the gelatine. Salt particles take the place of the water molecules joined to the gelatine molecules. The gummy candy loses water molecules and it shrinks to a smaller size.

LIQUID LAYERS

Your kitchen is full of forces that are hard at work. In this experiment, discover an awesome balance of forces that makes things float or sink.

 MESS WARNING!
Food coloring stains—
wear old clothes!

1 Add a few drops of food coloring to a small glass of water to make a nice strong color. Stir the mixture.

2 Pour ½ inch (1.2 cm) of golden syrup into a tall glass. Then add ½ inch (1.2 cm) of glycerine, ½ inch (1.2 cm) of colored water, and ½ inch (1.2 cm) of olive oil. The liquids will separate into layers.

3 Carefully put a split pea onto the surface of the olive oil.

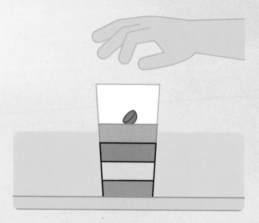

4 Time how long it takes the split pea to sink through each layer of liquid. What do you notice?

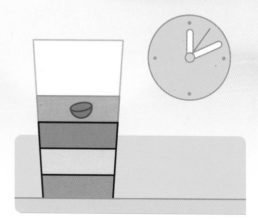

You will need...

- Glycerine
- Food coloring
- Golden syrup
- Split peas
- Tall glass
- Small glass
- Teaspoon
- Olive oil
- Ruler
- Watch with a second hand

If you don't have a split pea, try using a lentil or a raisin— or experiment with both to see what happens.

The Science: FLOATING AND DENSITY

This experiment has several floating liquid layers. Each layer floats because it's less **dense** than the layer underneath.

Denser substances contain more matter for their volume than less dense substances. They also push back harder when you press on them. Your split pea sank more slowly through the denser liquid layers because these layers pushed back harder than the less dense layers.

The force of a liquid pushing up is called upthrust. When the split pea settles on a layer, the upthrust force exactly balances the weight of the split pea. The speed at which the pea falls through a layer depends on the density of the liquid and how viscous (thick) the liquid is.

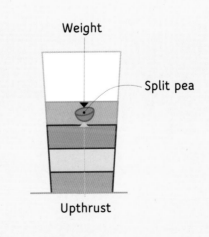

Weight

Split pea

Upthrust

FLOATING FACT-FINDER

You don't need fancy science equipment to measure the density of liquids. All you need is a drinking straw and some adhesive putty!

1 Fill two glasses with warm water to within 1 inch (2.5 cm) of the top.

2 Stir 5 teaspoons of salt into one glass. Stir the mixture until all the salt has dissolved. Fill the third glass with cooking oil to within 1 inch (2.5 cm) of the top.

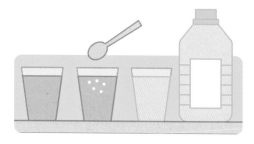

3 Cut a 5 cm length of drinking straw. Make a ball of adhesive putty about ½ inch (1.2 cm) across and mold it over and around the end of the straw so that it blocks the hole.

4 Place the straw upright in the fresh water, putty-end down. Use a waterproof marker to mark the water level on the straw. Now put the straw into the salty water and mark the water level again.

The Science: FLOATING AND SINKING

You've made a hydrometer! This instrument measures how dense a liquid is compared with water.

Imagine you're swimming. Your weight pulls you down into the water, but the force of upthrust pushes you up (see page 79).

You will need...

- Three identical small glasses
- Cooking oil
- Adhesive putty
- Drinking straws
- Ruler
- Salt
- Teaspoon
- Waterproof marker

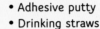

5 Finally, put the straw upright into the cooking oil. Mark the oil level on the straw. Does it float higher or lower than in the fresh water?

The two forces are roughly equal, which is why it's quite hard to sink to the bottom of a swimming pool.

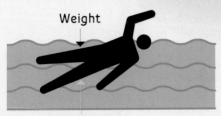

Weight

Upthrust

Dense liquids have greater upthrust, which means objects float higher in them. Salty water is denser than fresh water and has greater upthrust, so your hydrometer floats higher in salty water. Cooking oil is less dense than fresh water, so its upthrust is weaker and your hydrometer floats lower. Do you think it would be easier or harder to swim in cooking oil?

RESTLESS RAISINS

Raisins don't take swimming lessons, but they are great swimmers! Try this experiment to see them in action...

1 Pour a glass of soda.

2 Add 10 raisins to the glass.

3 What happens to the raisins?

4 Now fill a screw-top jar with soda and add 10 raisins. Close the lid and give the jar a shake.

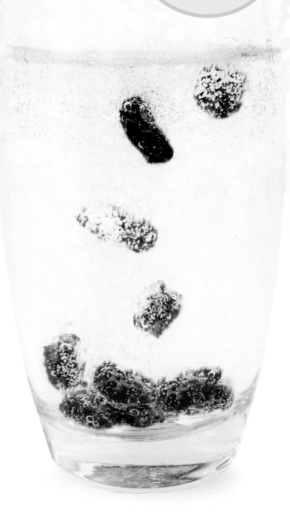

Use soda from a new bottle that hasn't been opened before.

You will need...

- Screw-top jar
- Tall glass
- Raisins
- Fizzy lemon-lime soda
- Tablespoon

The Science: FLOATING AND BUOYANCY

An object's weight acts downwards, and when in a liquid, an upthrust force acts upwards on it (see pages 79 and 81). In fact, any object floats if the weight of liquid it pushes aside is equal to its own weight. The ability to float is called 'buoyancy'.

When you add raisins to the soda, they sink because they're heavier than the soda they push aside.

But like any fizzy drink, lemon-lime soda contains dissolved **carbon dioxide** gas. In the bottle, the gas doesn't form bubbles because the liquid is under pressure. When you open the bottle, you release the pressure and bubbles of gas appear.

When you add the raisins, bubbles form on the rough surface of the raisins. The gas bubbles make the raisins lighter than the volume of soda they are pushing aside, so the raisins rise to the surface. Then the bubbles burst, making the raisins heavier, so they sink.

In step 5, the raisins in the jar became less active after a few minutes because, 1) after you released some of the gas, there was less gas to make bubbles; and 2) with the lid on, the pressure on the remaining bubbles stopped them from growing big enough to raise the raisins.

5 Loosen the lid to release some of the gas, then tighten it so that no more gas can escape. Watch the raisins for a few minutes. Which raisins were most active, those in the jar or those in the glass? Check out The Science (right) to find out why the raisins behaved differently.

KITCHEN BAG CHALLENGE

Getting a bag out of a jar should be easy, right? So why is this task impossible? Blame the air!

1 Take a plastic bag, put it over the top of a glass jar and secure it with wide sticky tape or masking tape. Pull the tape tight to make an airtight seal.

3 Now place the plastic bag inside the jar and fold the top down over the outside of the jar. Wrap sticky tape tightly around the bag to secure it.

2 Try to push the bag into the jar. Sounds easy? But it really isn't! OK, remove the bag and tape from the jar.

4 Now try to pull the bag out from inside the jar. What happens?

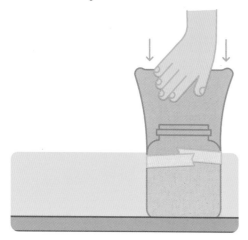

You will need...

- Scissors
- Clean plastic food bag
- Wide clear tape or masking tape

The Science: AIR PRESSURE

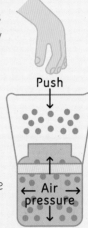

In step 1, the jar appears to be empty, but actually it's full of air molecules. When you try to push the bag into the jar, the air molecules are squashed together. The harder you push, the harder the air molecules push back. It's impossible to push the bag into the jar! The force of air pressing on a surface is called air pressure.

Push

← Air →
pressure

When you try to pull the bag out of the jar, you're fighting against air pressure pressing on the bag. The force of the air pressure is so strong that it's impossible to pull the bag out from the jar.

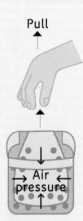

Pull

→ Air ←
pressure

DID YOU KNOW?

Air pressure is amazingly strong. In fact, the air pressure on your head is equal to carrying around a small car! Your body can withstand the pressure, and you don't notice it because it's always there.

WATERY WONDERS

Water isn't colorless and boring—it's got hidden depths. You can even make it do tricks without getting your hands wet!

1 Fill the plastic tub with water. Hold both jars completely underwater at an angle on their sides so that all the air escapes from inside them.

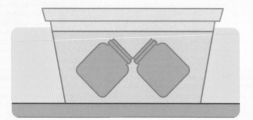

2 Bring the jars together, rim to rim, under the water.

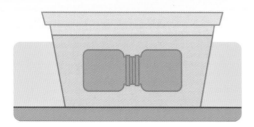

3 Still holding the two jars together, carefully lift them from the bowl. Stand the two jars on the tray as shown. Try not to spill any water. Dry your hands.

4 Holding the lower jar steady, slide the upper jar a tiny bit to one side to leave a very small gap. You may need help to do this.

 ASK AN ADULT

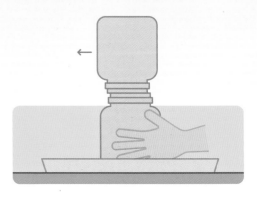

You will need...

- Large plastic tub
- Cotton cloth or tea towel
- Drinking straw
- Water
- Two identical large plastic tub
- Large tray with high sides
- Ribbon or rubber band
- Glass

5 Hold the drinking straw so it points at the small gap between the jars. The end of the straw should be about change to ½ inch (1.2 cm) away from the gap. Blow gently through the drinking straw. What happens?

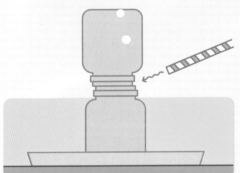

6 Now for a different trick! Fill one of the jars to the brim with water and cover it with a cotton cloth. The water may soak through the fabric. Tie a ribbon tightly around the top of the jar so the fabric can't move at all.

7 Gently turn the jar upside down. What happens this time?

If you don't have a large plastic tub, any large bowl will do. Instead of a tray, you could use a roasting dish.

The Science:
SURFACE TENSION

Because water molecules are drawn together. The surface of water acts like a thin, stretchy skin. This is called 'surface tension'. The stretchy skin allows water to form into drops. It is even strong enough for some insects and spiders to walk on it.

Using the straw you can blow air with enough force to break through the surface tension. The air forms bubbles. The bubbles float up and merge to form an air space with enough air pressure to push water from the top jar. If you blow enough air into the water, you can empty all the water from the top jar without touching the jars!

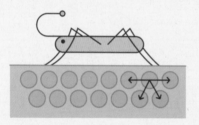

As you pull the two jars slightly apart, surface tension stops the water from leaking out. But surface tension isn't very strong. If you move the jars too far apart, you will break the surface tension and water will leak from the gap between the jars.

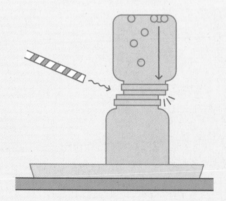

Steps 7 and 8 once more show surface tension in action. Like paper (see page 73), cotton consists of cellulose fibers. Water molecules are attracted to the fibers. Surface tension makes water push upwards between the fibers, but stops it from escaping from the fibers. This is why the water doesn't pour out when you turn the jar upside down.

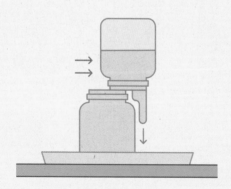

DID YOU KNOW?

On Earth you rarely find round drops of water because air resistance distorts them. But in space, where air resistance is weaker, surface tension pulls a drop into a perfectly round ball.

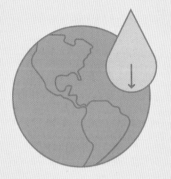

Watery wonder challenges:
CAN YOU FIGURE THEM OUT?

1 Fill a glass with water and lower a paper clip onto the water surface end-on. Now lay another paper clip flat on the water's surface. Why does one paper clip sink and the other float? Clue: look at the surface through a magnifying glass and think of the paper clip's weight pressing on the water's surface.

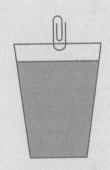

2 Very carefully pour some water into a glass until it reaches the very top. Look at the surface closely. Why does the water bulge above the rim of the glass?

Answer 1:

Surface tension supports the paper clip when you lay it flat on the water, but it's not strong enough to bear the weight of the end-on paper clip.

Answer 2:

As the water reaches the top of the glass, surface tension tries to stop it spilling over the rim. Instead the water's surface bulges upwards.

SINK OR SWIM?

Two balls of paper go for a swim. One ball sadly sinks and the other surprisingly swims, but why?

1 Draw and cut out two paper squares measuring 1 x 1 inch (2.5 x 2.5 cm).

2 Screw each piece of paper into a ball about ¾ inch (2 cm) across.

¾ inch (2 cm)

3 Fill two identical glasses with exactly the same amount of water.

4 Gently dribble a tablespoon of dishwashing liquid into the water in one of the glasses.

This is a comparison experiment. By using two glasses of water that are identical except for the dishwashing liquid, you know it must be the dishwashing liquid that affects the result.

You will need...

- Paper
- Pencil
- Two identical glasses
- Tablespoon
- Ruler
- Scissors
- Dishwashing liquid
- Hand whisk
- Water

5 Using a hand whisk, gently swirl the water. Try not to make bubbles or spill any water. The water will take on the color of the dishwashing liquid.

6 Lower a paper ball into each glass of water. What happens to the paper balls? Find out why in the box below.

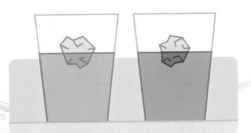

The Science:
DETERGENT AND WATER TENSION

You might think that the water would soak into both paper balls equally, increasing their density and making them sink to the bottom of the glasses. But the ball in fresh water floats! Surface tension between the water molecules holds them together and slows down the water from seeping into the cracks in the paper ball.

Dishwashing liquid contains detergent molecules. One end of a molecule of detergent pulls on a molecule of water. The detergent molecule tugs the water molecule away from the other water molecules. This breaks the surface tension around the paper ball, so the water soaks into the cracks until it's dense enough to sink.

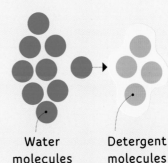

Water molecules   Detergent molecules

WHIRLING WHIRLPOOL

Whirling whirlpools suck people to a watery doom. You can make a miniature whirlpool of your own, but don't panic! Yours will be locked in a bottle.

1 Fill a measuring cup with water. Pour the water into a plastic bottle until it is three-quarters full.

2 Add four drops of food coloring. Put the lid on the bottle and shake to mix. .

3 Remove the lid of the bottle and add enough olive oil to make a layer ½ inch (1.2 cm) thick.

4 Put the lid back on tight. Hold the sides of the bottle and move it in circles as fast as you can. Look for your whirlpool!

DID YOU KNOW?

Vortices (more than one vortex) are spinning masses of air or water, and they are surprisingly common. You'll find them:

- In tornadoes, which are violent air vortices
- Behind the wings of a plane as it flies through the air
- In storms on other planets, such as the Great Red Spot on the planet Jupiter
- In a bath, as water goes down the plughole

You will need...

- Olive oil
- Ruler
- Measuring cup
- Liquid food coloring or glitter
- Tablespoon
- 16.9 ounce (500 ml) plastic or glass bottle with screw cap or cork
- Water

If you need to remove any labels from the bottle, ask an adult to soak it in hot, soapy water and then scrub them off.

5 Put the bottle down and watch what happens to the oil.

The Science: A VORTEX

Your miniature whirlpool is a spinning funnel, or vortex, of oil that forms in the water.

Swirling the bottle around causes the water and oil to spin in the bottle. Water is denser than olive oil and is thrown towards the sides of the bottle. Olive oil and air fill in the space in the middle of the water, forming a vortex.

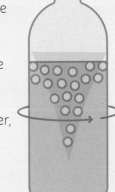

A SMASHING EXPERIMENT!

Here's how to freak out your friends with an amazing trick and NOT get grounded for smashing the best china!

1 Completely clear the table. Place a large sheet of shiny wrapping paper on the table like a tablecloth.

2 On the wrapping paper, lay the table for two people with plastic cups, plates or bowls and spoons.

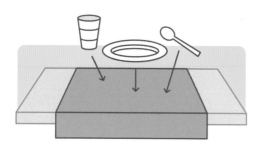

3 Put a mandarin on/in each plastic plate or bowl and in each cup.

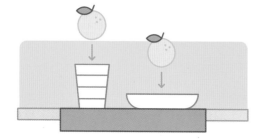

4 Stand at arm's length from the table. Pinch the wrapping paper and gently pull it towards you. What happens?

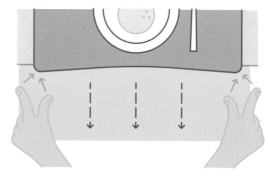

5 Now pull the wrapping paper as fast and smoothly as you can. It should come right out from under the plates or bowls, spoons and cups, leaving them standing!

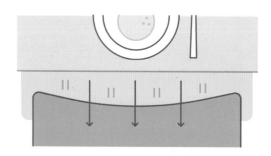

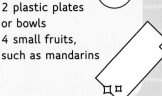

The Science:
INERTIA

Sir Isaac Newton's First Law of Motion says that an object will stay still or move in a straight line until an unbalanced force acts on it. The quality that makes an object do this is called **inertia**.

When you pull the wrapping paper gently, a rubbing force called **friction** keeps the objects on the wrapping paper. They move with the paper. But the force of friction between the objects and the wrapping paper is quite weak.

When you pull the paper quickly, the force of your pull overcomes the force of friction. You're able to pull the wrapping paper off the table, but the inertia of the plates or bowls, spoons and cups keeps them where they were.

CHAPTER 8: COLORFUL CHEMISTRY
MILKY MARVELS

Kitchen science is all about chemistry, and it can get pretty colorful! Have fun making bright, swirling patterns and discover why they happen.

⚠ **MESS WARNING!**
Food coloring stains—
wear old clothes!

1 Pour just enough milk into a bowl to cover the bottom.

2 Pour a blob of dishwashing liquid onto a saucer. Roll one end of a cotton swab in the dishwashing liquid.

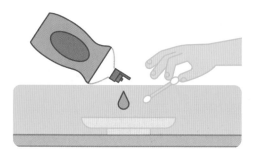

3 Use a paintbrush to add 2-3 drops of food coloring to the milk. The color may start to merge with the milk.

4 Quickly touch the milk with the end of the cotton swab that you dipped in the dishwashing liquid.

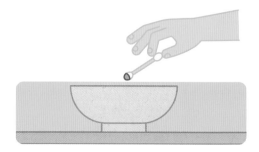

5 Repeat steps 3 and 4 using different shades of food coloring. Have fun making lots of swirling patterns.

Try this experiment several times. You might like to photograph your results! Try using different kinds of milk, or milk at different temperatures. Which combination of milk and temperature gives the best results?

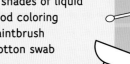

You will need...

- Shallow bowl or dish
- Saucer
- 2% milk
- Dishwashing liquid
- 3 shades of liquid food coloring
- Paintbrush
- Cotton swab

The Science:
SWIRLING LIQUIDS AND MIXING

The colors swirl out across the milk, but why? Milk consists of fat, protein and vitamin molecules floating in water. The water in milk has surface tension, just like fresh water.

Dishwashing liquid is a detergent, and as you found out on page 91, one end of a detergent molecule grabs a water molecule. This breaks the surface tension of water. But detergent molecules have another trick up their sleeve. The other end of the detergent molecule grabs a fat molecule.

When you add the dishwashing liquid, the detergent molecules break the surface tension of the milk and create currents in it. As the water and food coloring molecules are pushed aside, the colors form fabulous swirling patterns.

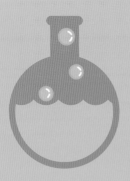

QUICK-CHANGE ACT

How can you make a liquid change color in your kitchen? All you need is a little chemistry...

> **WARNING!**
> Don't drink the baking soda and grape juice mixture. It could make you feel sick.

1 Add ½ cup (120 ml) of red grape juice to each glass.

2 Add two teaspoons of baking soda to one of the glasses and stir well.

3 Compare the colors of the liquids. What has happened?

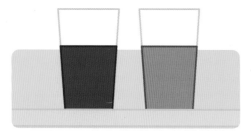

You will need...

- Red grape juice
- Baking soda
- Teaspoon
- Two identical clear glasses
- Measuring cup

The Science:
ACIDS, BASES, INDICATORS AND COLORS

Grape juice contains an acid chemical. When you combine a strong acid with water, the acid dissolves other substances. Luckily the acid in grape juice isn't strong enough to harm you! Baking soda is a weak **alkali**— an alkali is a type of **base** that dissolves in water. A strong alkali dissolved in water can dissolve other substances in a similar way to acids.

The alkali in the baking soda is strong enough to alter color molecules in the grape juice. As the molecules change, they reflect different colors of light. The liquid appears to change color to a dark blue-purple.

At the same time, bubbles appear. These are carbon dioxide gas bubbles produced by a **chemical reaction** between the alkaline baking soda and the acid in the grape juice.

Scientists measure how acidic a substance is using the pH scale. The lower the pH of a substance, the more acidic it is. Alkalis have a higher pH. A substance such as grape juice that changes color according to pH is called an indicator.

DID YOU KNOW?

Acids have a sour taste. The sour taste of lemon and vinegar are due to the acids they contain.

GIANT GREEN EGG

With just a little chemistry magic, you can turn a normal egg into a giant green egg—no giant green chickens involved! Turn the page to see the egg-stra-ordinary green egg.

MESS WARNING!
Food coloring stains—wear old clothes!
At step 6, handle the egg with care or it may burst!

2 Rest a dessert spoon on the egg to stop it floating and leave it in the vinegar for 24 hours, turning it occasionally. What happens to the egg?

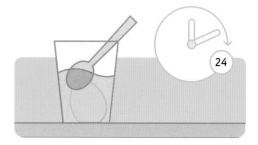

1 Gently place an egg into a glass. Pour ⅔ cup (160 ml) of white, cider or white wine vinegar over the egg.

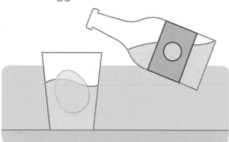

Turn the egg a few times in the vinegar so that the liquid is in contact with all areas of the eggshell.

3 Take the egg out of the vinegar, gently dry it with paper towel and drop it into the sink from a height of 1½ to 2 inches (4 to 5 cm). What happens?

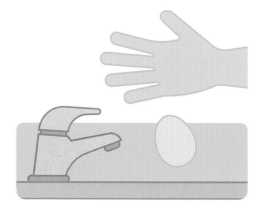

You will need...

- Egg
- Glass
- Measuring cup
- Two glass jars, 2 to 3 times bigger than the egg
- Green food coloring
- Saucer
- Sugar
- White, cider or white wine vinegar
- Dessert spoon
- Pencil
- Paper towel
- Water
- Cling film
- Flashlight

4 Take a glass jar two to three times bigger than the egg. Cover the bottom of the jar with sugar. Place the egg on the sugar and pour on more sugar until the egg is just covered.

5 Leave the egg in the sugar for a further 36 hours.

36

6 Carefully remove the egg and place it in a saucer. Gently press it with the blunt end of a pencil. What happens?

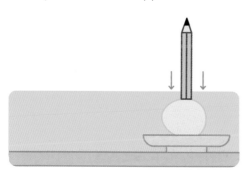

7 Take a clean glass jar and pour in some water. Add enough green food coloring to turn the water a strong, dark green.

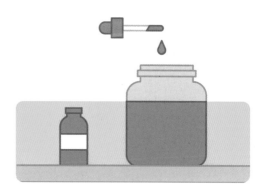

8 Gently wash the egg and place it in the green water. Leave it for 24 hours. Then, use the spoon to gently remove the egg from the water and place it on a saucer. How has the egg changed?

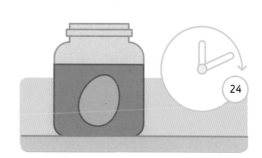

24

Try experimenting with other food colors. It's possible to make giant red, yellow and blue eggs, too!

The Science:
ACIDS AND OSMOSIS

This experiment combines two ways in which materials change—dissolving and osmosis.

Vinegar contains acid, and eggshells are mostly chalk, also known as calcium carbonate. The acid in the vinegar dissolves the calcium carbonate. The bubbles you see in step 2 are carbon dioxide gas produced by this chemical reaction.

After 24 hours, the eggshell has dissolved, leaving behind the rubbery inner layer of the egg. Because the surface is now rubbery, the egg bounces when you drop it!

Some chemical reactions can be reversed, but others, such as dissolving calcium carbonate, can't. Once you've dissolved the eggshell, you can't get it back!

After 36 hours in the sugar, the egg feels soft and saggy. You can make a dent in it if you gently press it with a pencil. Eggshells protect an egg from losing water, but without its shell, the egg loses water into the sugar by osmosis, leaving it saggy. The water that has come out of the egg turns the sugar into a gloopy syrup.

Thanks to the sugar, there isn't much water left in the egg. So when you place the egg in colored water, water soaks into it by osmosis and the egg swells to become a giant egg. Color molecules pass into the egg too, turning it green!

Egg challenge:
CAN YOU MAKE AN EGG GLOW IN THE DARK?

Take another egg and soak it in vinegar for 24 hours to dissolve its shell. You'll now be able to shine a light through it! Wait until dark, then set up the display as shown. The egg will appear to glow in the dark!

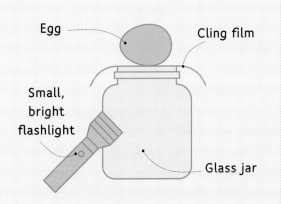

Egg

Cling film

Small, bright flashlight

Glass jar

FOAMY FUN

If there's one thing better than bubbles, it's LOADS OF BUBBLES. And if there's one thing better than loads of bubbles, it's LOADS OF COLORED BUBBLES! Here's how to make them.

MESS WARNING!
Food coloring stains fabrics. Put down newspaper and keep food coloring away from curtains and carpets.

WARNING!
If you have sensitive skin, try bubble bath instead of dishwashing liquid.

1 Measure ½ cup (120 ml) of water into a large bowl. Add two tablespoons of dishwashing liquid.

2 Add 10 drops of food coloring (all one color) to the mixture.

3 **ASK AN ADULT** Ask an adult to blend the mixture for 2 minutes or until the foam can be pushed into peaks. They can use either a powerful handheld blender or a food processor.

4 **ASK AN ADULT** If your helper used a food processor, ask them to pour the bubble mixture back into the large bowl. Tip the large bowl as shown so the foam stays on one side of the bowl.

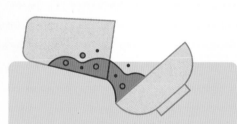

5 Repeat steps 1–4 using different food colorings. Try to keep the colored foam in separate segments in the bowl.

6 Now have fun swirling and mixing the colored foams. Notice how the colors change as you mix them.

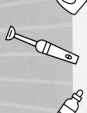
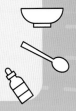

You will need...

- Food processor or powerful handheld blender (a small blender won't be powerful enough)

- Concentrated dishwashing liquid
- 3 or 4 shades of liquid food coloring, ideally red, green and blue

- Water
- Tablespoon
- Large bowl
- Measuring cup

The Science:
MIXING BUBBLES AND COLORS

Water bubbles burst quickly because surface tension is always pulling the water molecules together, and away from air. But dishwashing liquid contains detergent molecules. Since one end of a detergent molecule grabs a water molecule (see page 91), you can mix detergent and water in thin layers. The layers surround trapped air to make longer-lasting bubbles!

When you mix different colors of foam, you might think the foam would get darker, but it actually gets paler. That's because the colors in the foam are really colored light reflecting from color molecules. Just like sunlight (see page 75), white light is a mixture of all colors. So the more colors you mix, the whiter the foam appears.

The different colors will show up best under a bright light.

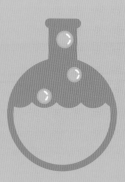

CRAZY LEMON VOLCANO

Want to turn a simple lemon into a mad, multi-colored volcano? Some colorful, chaotic chemistry can make that happen!

> ⚠ **MESS WARNING!**
> Food coloring stains—wear old clothes!

1 Ask an adult to cut a lemon in half. Place one half, cut side facing up, onto a sheet of black paper. Keep the other half for step 6.

ASK AN ADULT

2 Use the pointed end of a pencil to make holes ½ inch (1.2 cm) deep around the edge of the cut surface of the lemon.

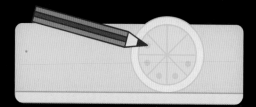

3 Put some water in a bowl. With a paintbrush, fill each hole with food coloring. Wash the brush in the water after each color.

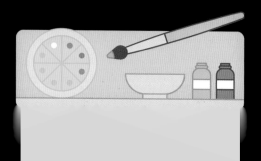

4 Pour a teaspoon of dishwashing liquid over the lemon flesh.

5 Sprinkle a few teaspoons of baking soda onto the cut lemon. Prod the flesh with the pencil.

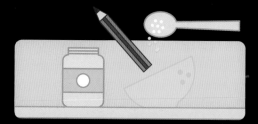

6 Squeeze a few drops of juice from the other half of the lemon onto the baking soda. Stand by for the eruption!

You will need...

- Lemon
- Knife
- Pencil
- Water
- Bowl
- Watercolor paintbrush
- Liquid food coloring (as many colors as you like)
- Dishwashing liquid
- 2 teaspoons
- Black paper
- Lemon juice
- Baking soda

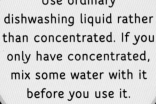

Use ordinary dishwashing liquid rather than concentrated. If you only have concentrated, mix some water with it before you use it.

The Science:
ACID AND ALKALINE

Lemon juice contains acid—usually about 6 percent citric acid—and baking soda is an alkali (see page 99). When you mix an acid and an alkali, you trigger a chemical reaction that produces **neutral** substances, in this case water, a salt called sodium citrate and carbon dioxide gas. A similar chemical reaction made carbon dioxide gas bubbles on an eggshell (page 100, step 2).

Mix detergent with water and air, and you make lots of bubbles. In this case the bubbles contain carbon dioxide gas, and the colors come from the food coloring!

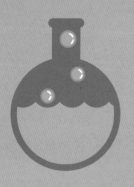

WEIRD TOAST

The previous chapter was all about chemistry without heat, but most kitchen chemistry uses heat—it's called cooking! Find out how to cook a simple piece of toast with a difference!

For your shape, instead of a toy figure you could use a cookie cutter or some cardstock into whatever shape you want.

1 Take a slice of white bread and wrap it tightly in cling film.

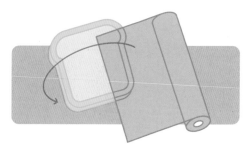

2 Press a toy figure or other shape into the bread. Press as hard as you can so the shape leaves a deep impression in the bread.

3 Remove the cling film. Ask an adult to set the toaster to its maximum setting, then toast the bread in the toaster.

ASK AN ADULT

4 Your shape should show clearly on the toast—and now you can eat it!

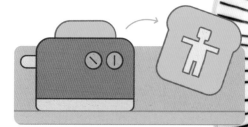

Bread browning challenge: DESIGN A MOLD

Can you make a bread design using toy building blocks? Arrange the blocks in a pattern on a plate. Press the cling film wrapped bread firmly onto the blocks, unwrap, then get toasting!

DID YOU KNOW?

Many foods, such as potatoes, meat and coffee, turn brown when you roast them. This is due to a chemical reaction called "browning".

The Science:
INFRARED LIGHT AND BROWNING

Inside your toaster, bread is blasted with a type of light called infrared light. You can't see infrared light, but you can feel it. On a sunny day, your skin feels warm due to infrared rays from the sun warming it up.

When anything heats up, its molecules have more energy and try to move around. Heat can also speed up chemical reactions, and that's what happens when you toast bread. Bread contains starch and protein. All starch and protein molecules are made up of smaller molecules. Starch is made of sugar molecules and protein is made of amino acids. The heat from the toaster triggers a chemical reaction on the surface of the bread between sugars and amino acids. This chemical reaction is called "browning". It results in the brown color and scent molecules that make a toasty smell.

The pressed areas appear paler because the pressed surface is smooth. The normally rough bits of bread dry out and become hotter than the smooth bits. The rough bits therefore brown more quickly.

If you heat your toast too much, it turns black as starch sugars combine with oxygen gas from the air. The black bits contain lumps of carbon.

MASSIVE MARSHMALLOWS

Did you know you can make a normal marshmallow grow to twice its normal size? Here's how you do it!

WARNING!
Microwaved marshmallows get VERY HOT inside. Do NOT try to eat one until it has cooled!

1 See how far you can stretch a marshmallow without breaking it. Measure the length of the stretched marshmallow.

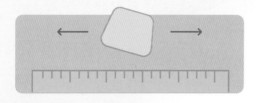

2 Fold a square of paper towel in four and put it on a plate. Place a marshmallow (not the stretched one!) on the paper towel. Ask an adult to microwave it for 40 seconds. Stand back and watch it through the window to see what happens.

ASK AN ADULT

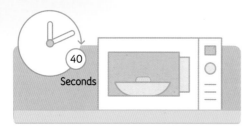

40 Seconds

3 Allow the cooked marshmallow to cool for two minutes. What happens to it as it cools? Measure the height and width of the cooked marshmallow and an uncooked one. Write down the figures.

You will need...

- Plate
- Microwave oven
- Marshmallows
- Ruler
- Notebook and pencil
- Paper towel

The Science:
AIR PRESSURE AND CARMELIZING

Marshmallows are soft, light and fluffy because they contain lots of tiny air bubbles. At least 50 percent of a marshmallow is air!

You can stretch unheated marshmallows because they contain a substance made from gelatine (see page 77). Gelatine is very stretchy.

As a marshmallow gets hotter, it gets larger. Inside the bubbles, heated air molecules push outwards more strongly. As the bubbles grow, the sweets swell. The hot marshmallow also starts to melt, because heat weakens the bonds linking the molecules in the gelatine and sugar.

The heat kick-starts a chemical reaction called "caramelization." Like browning (see page 109), caramelization makes food brown and tasty, but this time the reaction breaks down sugar molecules and releases water. After two minutes in the microwave, the marshmallow will start to caramelize and turn brown.

4 Ask an adult to place another marshmallow in the microwave, this time for two minutes. How does this marshmallow compare to an uncooked one?

ASK AN ADULT

CREATING CARAMEL

Take some sugar, add a bit of kitchen chemistry and make your very own yummy caramel. What's not to like?

 WARNING!
The sugar mixture gets VERY hot Keep clear and beware spills! Do NOT try to eat it before it has cooled!

1 Pour half a tablespoon of oil into the saucepan and smear it around with a paper towel.

2 Measure ¼ cup (50 g) of white sugar and put it in the saucepan.

3 Add two tablespoons of water and 4-5 drops of lemon juice.

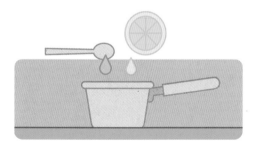

4 Pour a little over 1.5 ounces (50 ml) of heavy cream into a measuring cup.

5 Ask an adult to heat the sugar mixture, moving the pan so that the mixture swirls around and heats evenly. The mixture needs to boil until it turns brown.

ASK AN ADULT

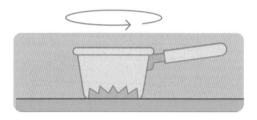

6 Once the mixture is a dark, sweet-smelling amber color, ask an adult to pour in the cream and briefly stir the mixture.

ASK AN ADULT

7 The adult should then remove the pan from the heat. When the mixture is cool, spread it on some bread or try it with ice cream—mmm!

ASK AN ADULT

You will need...

- Heavy cream
- Lemon juice
- Cooking oil
- Tablespoon
- Kitchen scales
- White sugar
- Saucepan
- Measuring cup
- Hand whisk
- Paper towel
- Water

Hot sugar sticks to things. Ask an adult to boil some water and pour it over every item that needs cleaning. This will loosen the sugar.

The Science: EVAPORATION, CARAMELIZATION AND CRYSTALS

As you heat the sugar and water, some of the water forms a gas called water vapor. This process is called **evaporation**. Water exists as solid ice, liquid water and water vapor. What form you get depends on how hot or cold the water is.

Heating also turns the sugar from a solid into a liquid. The caramelization chemical reaction (see page 111) then turns the sugar a lovely brown color. You wiped the saucepan with oil and added lemon juice to the mixture to stop sugar **crystals** forming in the caramel and making it gritty.

DID YOU KNOW?

Dark caramel gives gravies and cola drinks a rich brown color.

VOLCANO ROCKS

Have fun bubbling up some edible volcanic rock without blowing up your kitchen or filling your home with hot ash...

WARNING!
This is a hot sugar experiment. Keep clear of the hot mixture and do NOT eat it before it has cooled!

1 Put a little margarine or butter on a square of paper towel and wipe it over a baking tray.

2 Add ¾ cup (150 g) of caster sugar to a saucepan. Add four tablespoons of golden syrup. Ask an adult to heat the mixture gently and stir it until the sugar melts.

ASK AN ADULT

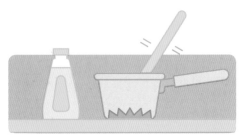

3 Let the mixture boil until it starts to darken. Ask an adult to take the saucepan off the heat and stir in two teaspoons of baking soda. What happens to the mixture?

ASK AN ADULT

4 Taking care to avoid spills, your adult helper should pour the mixture onto the baking tray. Allow the mixture to cool. Before you break it into bite-size pieces, what do you notice about the way it looks?

ASK AN ADULT

DID YOU KNOW?

Baking soda is found naturally in natron, the mineral used to preserve Egyptian mummies. It's also used to treat indigestion.

You will need...

- Caster sugar
- Kitchen scales
- Tablespoon
- Golden syrup
- Deep saucepan
- Wooden spoon
- Baking soda
- Teaspoon
- Baking tray
- Margarine or butter
- Paper towel

The Science:
BAKING SODA AND VOLCANOES

When you added baking soda, it made the mixture bubble madly. The bubbles contain carbon dioxide gas.

Baking soda is an alkali, and you normally need to mix it with an acid to make carbon dioxide gas (see page 107). But in this experiment, the heat breaks up the baking soda molecules to produce carbon dioxide gas without any need for an acid.

The carbon dioxide gas bubbles get trapped in the cooling mixture and look just like the bubbles in some volcanic rocks. In volcanic rocks, the bubbles are formed by dissolved gas and steam when the rock is still hot and molten. Molten rock that has erupted from a volcano is called "lava."

MASHED-UP MOONS

Here's how to make your very own alien moons using mashed potato. Smashing!

Although the instructions are for four potato balls you can make as many as you like!

1 Wash your hands. Grease the baking tray with a little butter—this will help to stop the moons sticking to the tray.

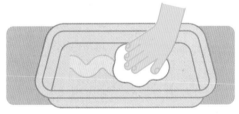

2 Put ¼ cup (about 50 g) of instant potato mixture into a bowl. Your adult helper should then add just enough boiling water to make a firm mixture.

ASK AN ADULT

3 Stir the mashed potato—it should be a little drier than you would make it if you were eating it as mash. Leave it to cool for 30 minutes.

WARNING!
Mashed potato gets very hot. Let it cool before you shape it!

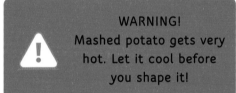

4 Roll the mash into four firm potato balls, or moons, about 3 inches (7.5 cm) across. Fill a glass with water and dip the teaspoon into it. Smooth the potato balls with the back of the wet teaspoon.

You will need...

- Baking sheet
- Butter
- Paper towel
- Packet of instant mashed potato
- Kitchen scales

- Bowl
- Grater
- Teaspoon
- Baking tray
- Glass
- Tablespoon

- Cheese
- Kettle
- Tomato ketchup
- Ruler
- Water
- Oven gloves

5 Grate enough cheese to cover two potato moons. Gently roll them in the cheese. You may need to re-shape them.

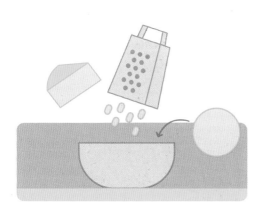

6 Use the back of the teaspoon to rub tomato ketchup over your other two potato moons.

⚠ MESS WARNING!
Don't forget to wash up afterwards!

7 Using a tablespoon, place the potato moons on the baking tray. Ask an adult to put the tray in the oven at 375°F (190°C) for 40 minutes, then take them out.

ASK AN ADULT

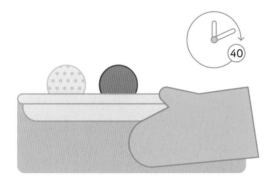

8 What do you notice about your alien moons? Have they changed size, and are they still round, or have alien forces been at work? Enjoy eating them!

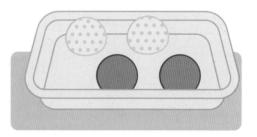

DID YOU KNOW?

The temperature at which cheese melts depends on how much water it contains. Very soft, watery cheeses, such as mozzarella, melt at a lower temperature than harder, drier cheeses such as Cheddar.

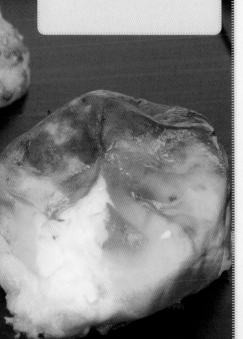

The Science:
COOKING CHEMISTRY, MOONS AND CHEESE

In the oven, the browning chemical reaction (see page 109) turns the potato and cheese a golden brown color. But first the cheese melts. Cheese is curdled milk and it contains milk fat and protein. As the cheese gets hotter, the fat droplets and the bonds holding protein molecules together break apart. The cheese turns into a gooey liquid. As the cheese cools, it becomes solid again.

Moons are natural objects that orbit (go around) planets. Earth's Moon isn't made of cheese, but there's one moon in our Solar System that really does look cheesy! It's called Io, and it orbits the planet Jupiter. Just as your edible alien moons are covered in hot, melted cheese, so parts of Io are covered in hot, molten rock, or lava, which comes from giant volcanoes.

Earth's Moon has no active volcanoes and most of the time it looks like your uncooked potato moons. But sometimes it turns red like a ketchup moon! This happens when Earth passes between the Sun and the Moon, and you see Earth's shadow on the Moon's surface. The red color is sunlight that passed through Earth's atmosphere (see page 75). We see it as red because the Moon reflects the red light back to Earth.

Io

Earth's Moon

CHAPTER 10: EASY FREEZY!
NICE CREAM

Question: What's nicer than a delicious dish of ice cream? Answer: a delicious dish of homemade scientific ice cream! Let's make some!

WARNING!
Handling ice can burn fingers. Ask your adult helper to wear gloves.

1 Pour ½ cup (120 ml) of heavy cream into a measuring cup. Add ½ cup (120 ml) of milk, one tablespoon of sugar and half a teaspoon of vanilla essence. Pour the mixture into the smaller bag. Seal the bag and shake it.

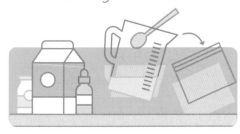

2 Ask an adult to half-fill a medium resealable plastic bag with ice cubes and hit it with a rubber mallet to crush the ice.

ASK AN ADULT

3 Add eight tablespoons of salt to the crushed ice. Place the smaller bag with the ice-cream mixture inside the medium bag and seal the medium bag. Place the medium bag inside a second medium resealable plastic bag and seal this too.

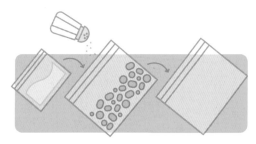

4 Wearing gloves, shake and squish the bags with your fingers for 12 minutes or until all the ice has melted in the medium bag. The longer you shake and squish, the creamier the mixture will become.

You will need...

- Gloves
- Tea towel
- Salt
- Heavy cream
- Whole milk
- Vanilla essence
- Dessert spoon
- Plastic container
- Ice cubes
- Caster sugar
- Tablespoon
- Teaspoon
- Plastic bowl
- Measuring cup
- 2 medium resealable plastic bags
- 1 small resealable plastic bag
- Rubber mallet

5 Open the two medium bags and lift out the smaller bag. Rinse the salt off it and turn out the ice cream into a plastic container. Pop some in a bowl to eat, or use it to make the recipe on pages 122–125.

The Science:
ICE CREAM: FREEZING AND MIXING

We know salt makes ice melt faster. Melting requires heat, so as the ice melts, it draws heat from the small bag. This makes the ice-cream mixture freeze.

You shake and squish the mixture to mix the ingredients. Squishing ensures that the ice crystals in the ice cream are small, so the mixture is smoother and less grainy. Shaking mixes the sugar with the fat (in the cream and milk) and the protein (in the milk), giving a creamy texture. The sugar adds sweetness and, like salt, ensures that the ice cream melts more quickly. This means it isn't too cold when you eat it. If it was too cold, you wouldn't be able to taste it and it might hurt your mouth. Vanilla gives the ice cream its flavor. Shaking and squishing also mixes in air, which keeps your ice cream light.

BAKED ICE CREAM

Surely hot ice cream is against the laws of science? WRONG! Here's how to bake the impossible. You can have fun with the shape, too—see page 124!

1 Line a baking tray with aluminum foil.

2 Wash and dry your hands.

3 Place a cookie on the foil-covered tray. Alternatively you could use a flan case cut to about the same size as a cookie.

If your eggs have been stored in the fridge, take them out and leave them to warm up at room temperature for about two hours before you use them.

4 Take three fresh, room-temperature eggs. To separate the yolks and whites, crack an egg on the rim of a bowl and break it open over the jug. Spoon out the yolk without breaking it, and put it in a glass. Pour the egg white into the bowl.

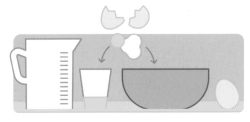

5 Repeat for each egg. Make sure NO egg yolk mixes with the whites.

6 Ask an adult to beat the mixture with an electric whisk for exactly 50 seconds. The egg whites will be very foamy.

ASK AN ADULT

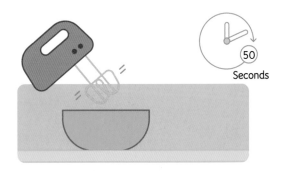

50 Seconds

You will need...

- Baking tray
- Aluminum foil
- Large, thick cookie
- Ice cream (not soft-scoop)

- 3 large eggs (ideally fresh eggs)
- Caster sugar
- Metal or glass bowl
- Jug

- Glass
- Electric whisk
- Kitchen scales
- Tablespoon
- Ice-cream scoop

7 Measure ⅔ cup (150 g) of caster sugar and add it to the egg whites, one tablespoon at a time. Ask your adult helper to carry on whisking at a slow speed until the mixture is glossy and forms very stiff peaks—this may take 10 minutes.

ASK AN ADULT

8 Place a dome-shaped scoop of ice cream on top of the cookie.

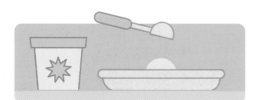

An ice-cream scoop is ideal for step 8. Do not use soft-scoop ice cream. Instead of shop-bought ice cream you could use your homemade ice cream from pages 120-121!

9 Cover the ice cream and cookie completely in egg white mixture. Take care not to leave any gaps.

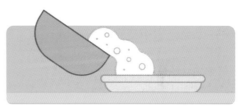

10 Place the dessert in the freezer for at least one hour.

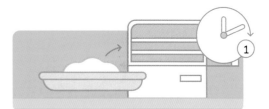

11 Ask an adult to set the oven to 450°F (230°C) and put the dessert in the hot oven. He or she should take it out after about five minutes, once the mixture has browned slightly.

ASK AN ADULT

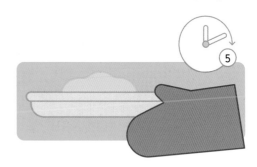

You could use cake stickers for your creature's feet and eyes—you can buy cake stickers from kitchen stores—or you could make them from icing.

CHILLY CREATURE CHALLENGE

Can you make a cooked ice-cream creature like this one? You can make the spikes by dipping the back of your spoon into the meringue and lifting it up. (Don't forget to check at step 7 that the mixture is forming very stiff peaks.)

124

The Science:
PROTEIN AND INSULATORS

So why hasn't the ice cream melted in the hot oven? And what has happened to the egg white mixture? Let's start with the egg white, which is about 92 percent water and 8 percent protein. The proteins are made up of chains of amino acids (see page 109)—each protein is like a ball of string floating in water. The outer layers of string are amino acids attracted to water, and on the inside are amino acids that push away water. Whisking the egg white mixes in air. Since some amino acids push away water, air bubbles get trapped among the amino acids. The protein molecules start to unravel, but then knit together in a kind of mesh around the bubbles.

Next you added sugar. The sugar dissolves in the egg white foam and thickens the mixture, making it stretchy. Heating makes a lot of water evaporate, but the protein mesh and stretchy mixture keeps the bubbles in place. In fact, heating makes the bubbles stronger by tightening the bonds linking the protein molecules. The heat is enough to trigger the browning chemical reaction (see page 109) on the outside of the meringue.

The meringue bubbles stop the ice cream from melting. They contain air, and air doesn't let heat pass through it easily—it is a good **insulator**. The air bubbles protect the ice cream from the heat of the oven.

The final word:
EDIBLE SCIENCE

If you've just tried the experiments in this book, you'll know that food and drink are packed with crucial chemistry and surprising science just begging to be discovered. Why not cook up your very own edible experiments? It's your chance to enjoy science—and eat it too!

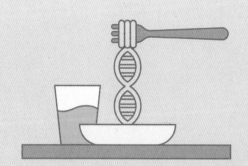

GLOSSARY

Acid: A type of chemical. When mixed with water, strong acids can dissolve other substances.

Air pressure: The atmosphere above us is pulled towards Earth by gravity. Air pressure is a force acting on an area caused by the weight of the air above us.

Alkali: A special kind of base that dissolves in water to make an alkaline solution. Like strong acids, strong alkaline solutions are able to dissolve other substances.

Angular momentum: The ability of a spinning object to keep spinning. Objects with lots of mass that are spinning quickly have a large angular momentum. Spinning makes an object such as a gyroscope more stable.

Base: A type of chemical that can neutralize acids.

Buoyant: Able to float or rise upwards in water. For this to happen, the upthrust of water must be greater or equal to the force of gravity pulling it down.

Carbon dioxide: A gas with molecules made up of a carbon atom and two oxygen atoms bonded together. Your body makes carbon dioxide in every living cell as it releases energy from food during respiration. We get rid of carbon dioxide in the air we breathe out.

Centrifugal effect: When an object is turned fast around an axis, it tries to move in a straight line at right angles to the axis. It's called an "effect" because it's not a real force.

Centripetal force: The force that pushes a turning object towards the axis of rotation. Without centripetal force, an object would move away in a straight line instead of turning.

Chemical reaction: The process when two or more chemicals combine to make a new molecule or molecules. Some chemical reactions can be reversed; others can't.

Condense: When a gas or vapor cools to form liquid droplets. Condensation is the opposite of evaporation.

Crystal: A substance where the atoms or molecules are arranged in a regular pattern. Crystals in your kitchen lab include salt, sugar and ice.

Dense/density: The amount of matter compared with the space it takes up. You can calculate the density of an object or a material by dividing its mass by its volume.

Drag: Form of friction produced when an object moves through gas or liquid.

Evaporate: When a liquid warms and its molecules escape in the form of gas.

Evaporation: When a liquid warms and turns to vapor. Puddles dry up because of evaporation.

Friction: The force created when two objects rub against each other. Friction often slows down moving objects and turns their energy into heat.

Inertia: The quality that keeps an object either still or moving in a straight line. The more matter an object contains, the more inertia it has.

Insulator: A material that heat or electricity cannot pass through easily.

Lift: Upward force produced when an object moves through a gas or liquid. Lift can overcome gravity. It helps flying objects gain height.

Mass: The amount of matter (material) that an object contains.

Molecule: Group of atoms bonded together. Most chemicals are made of molecules.

Momentum: The ability of a moving object to keep moving. Objects with lots of mass and speed have more momentum than lighter, slower objects.

Neutral: A chemical that isn't an acid or a base—it's in-between. Pure water is a neutral chemical.

Photosynthesis: How plants turn water and carbon dioxide gas into food using energy from sunlight. Oxygen gas is given off as a by-product.

GLOSSARY

Protein: A type of molecule made of chains of smaller molecules called amino acids. You need to eat protein in order to grow and stay healthy. Proteins are found in many foods and all animals and plants.

Species: A type of animal or plant that can breed successfully with its own kind.

Viscosity: How much a fluid resists attempts to stir it or make it change shape. Viscous liquids are thick and some appear almost solid.

Wavelength: Imagine a wavy line; wavelength is the gap between each peak.